# Photoshop CS6:
# Advanced
## Student Manual

### ACE Edition

# Photoshop CS6: Advanced

| | |
|---|---|
| **Chief Executive Officer, Axzo Press:** | Ken Wasnock |
| **Series Designer and COO:** | Adam A. Wilcox |
| **Vice President, Operations:** | Josh Pincus |
| **Director of Publishing Systems Development:** | Dan Quackenbush |
| **Writer:** | Chris Hale |
| **Keytester:** | Lori Minnehan |

## Trademarks

ILT Series is a trademark of Axzo Press.

Some of the product names and company names used in this book have been used for identification purposes only and may be trademarks or registered trademarks of their respective manufacturers and sellers.

## Disclaimer

We reserve the right to revise this publication and make changes from time to time in its content without notice.

ISBN 10: 1-4260-3553-5
ISBN 13: 978-1-4260-3553-1

Printed in the United States of America

1 2 3 4 5 GL 06 05 04 03

# Contents

# Introduction

After reading this introduction, you will know how to:

**A** Use ILT Series manuals in general.

**B** Use prerequisites, a target student description, course objectives, and a skills inventory to properly set your expectations for the course.

**C** Re-key this course after class.

# Topic A:  About the manual

### ILT Series philosophy

Our manuals facilitate your learning by providing structured interaction with the software itself. While we provide text to explain difficult concepts, the hands-on activities are the focus of our courses. By paying close attention as your instructor leads you through these activities, you will learn the skills and concepts effectively.

We believe strongly in the instructor-led class. During class, focus on your instructor. Our manuals are designed and written to facilitate your interaction with your instructor, and not to call attention to manuals themselves.

We believe in the basic approach of setting expectations, delivering instruction, and providing summary and review afterwards. For this reason, lessons begin with objectives and end with summaries. We also provide overall course objectives and a course summary to provide both an introduction to and closure on the entire course.

### Manual components

The manuals contain these major components:

- Table of contents
- Introduction
- Units
- Appendix
- Course summary
- Glossary
- Index

Each element is described below.

#### Table of contents

The table of contents acts as a learning roadmap.

#### Introduction

The introduction contains information about our training philosophy and our manual components, features, and conventions. It contains target student, prerequisite, objective, and setup information for the specific course.

#### Units

Units are the largest structural component of the course content. A unit begins with a title page that lists objectives for each major subdivision, or topic, within the unit. Within each topic, conceptual and explanatory information alternates with hands-on activities. Units conclude with a summary comprising one paragraph for each topic, and an independent practice activity that gives you an opportunity to practice the skills you've learned.

The conceptual information takes the form of text paragraphs, exhibits, lists, and tables. The activities are structured in two columns, one telling you what to do, the other providing explanations, descriptions, and graphics.

### Appendix

The appendix for this course lists the Adobe Certified Expert (ACE) exam objectives for Photoshop CS6, along with references to corresponding coverage in ILT Series courseware.

### Course summary

This section provides a text summary of the entire course. It is useful for providing closure at the end of the course. The course summary also indicates the next course in this series, if there is one, and lists additional resources you might find useful as you continue to learn about the software.

### Glossary

The glossary provides definitions for all of the key terms used in this course.

### Index

The index at the end of this manual makes it easy for you to find information about a particular software component, feature, or concept.

## Manual conventions

We've tried to keep the number of elements and the types of formatting to a minimum in the manuals. This aids in clarity and makes the manuals more classically elegant looking. But there are some conventions and icons you should know about.

| Item | Description |
|---|---|
| *Italic text* | In conceptual text, indicates a new term or feature. |
| **Bold text** | In unit summaries, indicates a key term or concept. In an independent practice activity, indicates an explicit item that you select, choose, or type. |
| `Code font` | Indicates code or syntax. |
| `Longer strings of ▶ code will look ▶ like this.` | In the hands-on activities, any code that's too long to fit on a single line is divided into segments by one or more continuation characters (▶). This code should be entered as a continuous string of text. |
| Select **bold item** | In the left column of hands-on activities, bold sans-serif text indicates an explicit item that you select, choose, or type. |
| Keycaps like (↵ ENTER) | Indicate a key on the keyboard you must press. |

## Hands-on activities

The hands-on activities are the most important parts of our manuals. They are divided into two primary columns. The "Here's how" column gives short instructions to you about what to do. The "Here's why" column provides explanations, graphics, and clarifications. Here's a sample:

*Do it!*

## A-1:   Creating a commission formula

| Here's how | Here's why |
|---|---|
| 1  Open Sales | This is an oversimplified sales compensation worksheet. It shows sales totals, commissions, and incentives for five sales reps. |
| 2  Observe the contents of cell F4 | F4 ▼ = =E4*C_Rate<br><br>The commission rate formulas use the name "C_Rate" instead of a value for the commission rate. |

For these activities, we have provided a collection of data files designed to help you learn each skill in a real-world business context. As you work through the activities, you will modify and update these files. Of course, you might make a mistake and therefore want to re-key the activity starting from scratch. To make it easy to start over, you will rename each data file at the end of the first activity in which the file is modified. Our convention for renaming files is to add the word "My" to the beginning of the file name. In the above activity, for example, a file called "Sales" is being used for the first time. At the end of this activity, you would save the file as "My sales," thus leaving the "Sales" file unchanged. If you make a mistake, you can start over using the original "Sales" file.

In some activities, however, it might not be practical to rename the data file. If you want to retry one of these activities, ask your instructor for a fresh copy of the original data file.

# Topic B: Setting your expectations

Properly setting your expectations is essential to your success. This topic will help you do that by providing:

- Prerequisites for this course
- A description of the target student
- A list of the objectives for the course
- A skills assessment for the course

## Course prerequisites

Before taking this course, you should be familiar with personal computers and the use of a keyboard and a mouse. Furthermore, this course assumes that you've completed the following courses or have equivalent experience:

- *Windows 7: Basic*
- *Photoshop CS6: Basic, ACE Edition*

## Target student

The target student for this course is familiar with the basics of using Adobe Photoshop to create and modify digital images, and wants to learn additional techniques for creating image effects.

### Adobe ACE certification

This course is designed to help you pass the Adobe Certified Expert (ACE) exam for Photoshop CS6. For complete certification training, you should complete this course and all of the following:

- *Photoshop CS6: Basic, ACE Edition*
- *Photoshop CS6: Production, ACE Edition*

## Course objectives

These overall course objectives will give you an idea about what to expect from the course. It is also possible that they will help you see that this course is not the right one for you. If you think you either lack the prerequisite knowledge or already know most of the subject matter to be covered, you should let your instructor know that you think you are misplaced in the class.

After completing this course, you will know how to:

- Group layers and clip layers, apply layer blending modes, use Smart Objects when creating a composite, and create and export layer comps.

- Specify colors and store them in the Swatches panel, apply colors to image selections and as fill layers, apply fill types such as gradients, use overlay layer styles to apply colors and gradients to layer content, select color in an image, adjust color, colorize an image, create a spot-color channel, and replace a color in an image.

- Paint in Quick Mask mode and in an alpha channel to specify a selection, create a layer mask to hide part of a layer, use grayscale masks to partially mask part of an image, and refine a selection by using the Refine Edge dialog box.

- Understand how vector layers differ from raster layers and when you might use a vector layer, use the path tools and commands to create vector paths and shapes, edit vector paths, and use paths to apply creative effects to type.

- Warp text and layers, use the Liquify filter to modify an image's pixels, use the Black & White options to convert an image to grayscale, convert a grayscale image to a duotone, apply filters as Smart Filters, and mask Smart Filters.

## Skills inventory

Use the following form to gauge your skill level entering the class. For each skill listed, rate your familiarity from 1 to 5, with five being the most familiar. *This is not a test.* Rather, it is intended to provide you with an idea of where you're starting from at the beginning of class. If you're wholly unfamiliar with all the skills, you might not be ready for the class. If you think you already understand all of the skills, you might need to move on to the next course in the series. In either case, you should let your instructor know as soon as possible.

| Skill | 1 | 2 | 3 | 4 | 5 |
|---|---|---|---|---|---|
| Grouping layers | | | | | |
| Clipping layers | | | | | |
| Filtering layers | | | | | |
| Applying layer blending modes | | | | | |
| Working with Smart Objects | | | | | |
| Creating and exporting layer comps | | | | | |
| Creating swatches | | | | | |
| Filling selections | | | | | |
| Creating fill layers | | | | | |
| Creating gradients | | | | | |
| Filling areas with overlay layer styles | | | | | |
| Selecting with the Magic Wand tool | | | | | |
| Selecting with the Color Range command | | | | | |
| Changing color by using adjustment layers | | | | | |
| Colorizing an image | | | | | |
| Adding a spot-color channel | | | | | |
| Replacing a color by painting | | | | | |
| Editing a Quick Mask | | | | | |
| Saving and loading a selection | | | | | |
| Creating a layer mask | | | | | |
| Creating a type mask | | | | | |

| Skill | 1 | 2 | 3 | 4 | 5 |
|---|---|---|---|---|---|
| Using the Refine Edge dialog box | | | | | |
| Creating a freeform path | | | | | |
| Converting a selection to a path | | | | | |
| Creating paths with the Pen tool | | | | | |
| Creating a vector shape layer | | | | | |
| Stroking a path with a brush shape | | | | | |
| Adjusting path points | | | | | |
| Converting type characters to editable shapes | | | | | |
| Wrapping type on a path | | | | | |
| Warping text | | | | | |
| Warping image layers | | | | | |
| Using Puppet Warp | | | | | |
| Using the Liquify filter | | | | | |
| Creating a grayscale image | | | | | |
| Creating a duotone | | | | | |
| Applying Smart Filters | | | | | |

# Topic C:  Re-keying the course

If you have the proper hardware and software, you can re-key this course after class. This section explains what you'll need in order to do so, and how to do it.

## Hardware requirements

Your personal computer should have:

- A keyboard and a mouse
- Intel Pentium 4 or AMD Athlon 64 Processor (or faster)
- 1GB RAM (or higher)
- 1 GB of available hard drive space after the operating system is installed
- A monitor with at least $1280 \times 960$ resolution
- A graphics display card chip (GPU) that supports OpenGL (**Note:** Activities will still work without OpenGL support, but some features won't be enabled.)

## Software requirements

You will also need the following software:

- Microsoft Windows 7 (You can also use Windows XP, but the screenshots in this course were taken in Windows 7, so your screens might look somewhat different.)
- Adobe Photoshop CS6
- A display driver that supports OpenGL 2.0 and Shader Model 3.0 (**Note:** Activities will still work without OpenGL support, but some features won't be enabled.)

## Network requirements

The following network components and connectivity are also required for re-keying this course:

- Internet access, for the following purposes:
    - Downloading the latest critical updates and service packs
    - Downloading the Student Data files (if necessary)

## Setup instructions to re-key the course

Before you re-key the course, you will need to perform the following steps.

1 Use Windows Update to install all available critical updates and Service Packs.

2 With flat-panel displays, we recommend using the panel's native resolution for best results. Color depth/quality should be set to High (24 bit) or higher.

Please note that your display settings or resolution may differ from the author's, so your screens might not exactly match the screen shots in this manual.

3 If necessary, reset any Photoshop defaults that you have changed. To do so, when starting Photoshop, hold down Shift+Ctrl+Alt until the dialog box appears, asking if you want to delete the settings file; click Yes. (If you do not wish to reset the defaults, you can still re-key the course, but some activities might not work exactly as documented.)

4 Configure Photoshop CS6 as follows:

a Start Photoshop.

b Choose Edit, Preferences, File Handling.

c Under File Compatibility, set Maximize PSD and PSB Compatibility to Always. Click OK.

d Close Photoshop.

5 If you have the data disc that came with this manual, locate the Student Data folder on it and copy it to the desktop of your computer.

If you don't have the data disc, you can download the Student Data files for the course:

a Connect to http://downloads.logicaloperations.com.

b Enter the course title or search by part to locate this course

c Click the course title to display a list of available downloads.
**Note:** Data Files are located under the Instructor Edition of the course.

d Click the link(s) for downloading the Student Data files.

e Create a folder named Student Data on the desktop of your computer.

f Double-click the downloaded zip file(s) and drag the contents into the Student Data folder.

# Unit 1

## Working with multiple layers

Complete this unit, and you'll know how to:

**A** Group layers and clip layers to underlying layers.

**B** Apply layer blending modes.

**C** Use Smart Objects when creating a composite.

**D** Create and export layer comps.

# Topic A:  Layer groups

This topic covers the following ACE exam objectives for Photoshop CS6.

| # | Objective |
|---|-----------|
| **5.4** | **Searching for layers** |
| 5.4.1 | Organizing documents that have many layers |
| 5.4.2 | Using the layer search feature |
| **5.5** | **Understanding layer groups** |
| 5.5.1 | Grouping Layers |
| 5.5.2 | Clipping Layers |
| 5.5.3 | Blend mode and masks using layer groups |
| 5.5.4 | Considerations for designs when using layer groups |
| 5.5.5 | Keyboard shortcuts for grouping layers |

## Compositing

*Explanation*

When you create an image by combining images—a process known as *compositing*—you can use several techniques to keep your workflow efficient. For example, you can group and link layers to organize the Layers panel and to manipulate multiple layers as a unit.

## Grouping layers

A *group* is a container in the Layers panel that can store multiple layers, as shown in Exhibit 1-1. You can expand a group so that all of its layers are listed in the Layers panel or collapse the group to hide its list of layers. You can adjust the group's blending mode or opacity to apply those settings to all layers in the group, and you can apply clipping masks to a group of layers. At the same time, you can still apply settings to the individual layers within the group.

To create an empty group with the default settings, click the "Create a new group" button in the Layers panel. The group will be named Group 1.

To create an empty group with settings you specify:

1  Open the New Group dialog box by doing either of the following:
   • From the Layers panel menu, choose New Group.
   • Press Alt and click the "Create a new group" button.
2  In the Name box, enter a name for the group.
3  Specify a color for the group icon, and specify a blending mode and opacity for the group.
4  Click OK.

To create a group containing selected layers and using the default settings, first select the layers you want to include in the group. Then drag the selected layers to the "Create a new group" button (or press Ctrl+G). The group will be named Group 1.

To create a group containing selected layers and using settings you specify:

1  Select the layers you want to store in the group.

2  Open the New Group from Layers dialog box:

   • From the Layers panel menu, choose New Group from Layers.

   • Press Alt and drag the layers to the "Create a new group" button.

3  Enter a name for the group.

4  Specify a color for the group icon, and specify a blending mode and opacity for the group.

5  Click OK.

To add a layer to an existing group in the Layers panel, drag the desired layer onto the group. To delete a group, select it and click the Delete layer button. In the alert box that appears, click Group and Contents to delete the group and its layers, or click Group Only to delete the group without deleting the layers within it.

You can nest layer groups by dragging one group into another, creating a hierarchy of folders in the Layers panel.

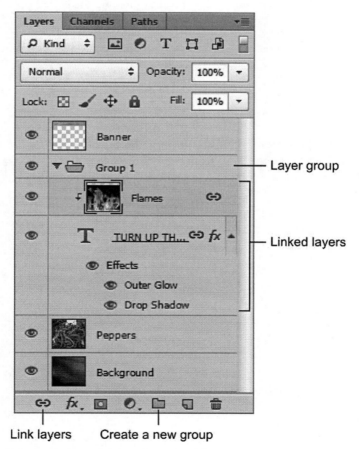

*Exhibit 1-1: Linked and grouped layers*

### Color-coding layers

If an image contains many layers, it can be difficult to find a specific one quickly. To help make certain ones stand out, you can apply a color that appears in the visibility column. This color appears only in the Layers panel and doesn't affect the layer's contents in the image.

To add a color to a layer, display the Layers panel menu and choose Layer Properties to open the Layer Properties dialog box. Select a color from the Color list and click OK. (You can also open the Layer Properties dialog box by choosing Layer, Layer Properties.)

### Locking layers

You can protect the content of layers by locking them, either partially or completely. To do so, in the Layers panel, select the desired layer and then select a lock option. The following table describes each layer lock option:

| Icon | Lock option | When the option is selected... |
|------|-------------|-------------------------------|
| ⊠ | Lock transparent pixels | You can edit only the opaque (non-transparent) areas of a layer. |
| ✎ | Lock image pixels | You can't modify the layer's pixels by using the painting tools. |
| ✛ | Lock position | You can't move the layer's content. |
| 🔒 | Lock all | All of the lock options are active. |

You can also apply lock options to multiple layers or to a layer group. To do so, select the layers or layer group; then, from the Layers panel menu, choose either Lock Layers or Lock All Layers in Group to open a dialog box. In the dialog box, select the desired lock options and click OK.

*Do it!*    **A-1:  Grouping layers**

The files for this activity are in Student Data folder **Unit 1\Topic A**.

| Here's how | Here's why |
|---|---|
| 1  Open Hot peppers 1 | |
| Save the image as **My hot peppers 1** | In the current topic folder. |
| 2  Select the TURN UP THE HEAT layer | |
| Press `CTRL` and click the Flames layer | To select both layers |
| 3  Press `CTRL` + `G` | To group the layers. |
| 4  Using the Move tool, drag in the image | To move both layers in the group at once. |
| Press `CTRL` + `Z` | To undo the move. |
| 5  Update the image | |

## Clipping masks

*Explanation*

When you create a *clipping mask*, you display the current layer over only the pixels in the layer below, as shown in Exhibit 1-2. The non-transparent areas in the layer below—the base layer—reveal the content of the layer above—the clipped layer.

Clipping masks work well when you want to mask a layer based on content that might change. For example, you can clip (attach) a layer to a type layer below it so that the clipping layer's contents are visible only over the text on the base layer. Because a clipping mask is dynamic, you can change the text in the layer below, and the effect is automatically updated.

A layer placed above a type layer

The flames layer clipped to the layer below it

*Exhibit 1-2: A clipping mask used with a type layer*

A clipping mask can contain more than two layers. All of the layers clip to the shape of the base layer. To create a clipping mask:

1 Move the layer that you want to create a clipping mask for so that it's directly above the layer whose content you want it to clip to.

2 To clip the layer to the base layer, do any of the following:

- Choose Layer, Create Clipping Mask.
- From the Layers panel menu, choose Create Clipping Mask.
- Press Alt, point between the two layers in the Layers panel, and click.

You can move the layers independently of one another. However, if you want them to move together, you can link them by selecting them both and clicking the Link layers button in the Layers panel.

To remove a clipping mask, you can use any of these techniques:

- Choose Layer, Release Clipping Mask.
- From the Layers panel menu, choose Release Clipping Mask.
- Press Alt, point to the line between the two layers in the Layers panel, and click.

### Linking layers

If you think you'll need to regularly manipulate a group of layers as a unit, you can link them. When layers are linked, their contents will always move as a unit, even if only one of the layers is selected.

To link layers, select the ones you want to link and then click the Link layers icon in the Layers panel. When you select a layer that's linked to other layers, a chain icon appears next to each of the linked layers in the Layers panel, as shown in Exhibit 1-1. If you want to remove a layer from a link, select that layer and click the Link layers icon.

*Do it!*

### A-2:   Clipping a layer to an underlying layer

| Here's how | Here's why |
|---|---|
| 1  In the Layers panel, expand the Group 1 layer group | <br><br>▼ 📁 Group 1<br><br>T   TURN UP THE H...  *fx* ▲<br><br>👁 Effects<br>👁 Outer Glow<br>👁 Drop Shadow<br><br>🔲 Flames |
| Drag the Flames layer above the TURN UP THE HEAT layer | You'll clip the Flames layer to the type layer below it, using the type layer as a clipping mask. |
| 2  Press ⟨CTRL⟩ + ⟨ALT⟩ + ⟨G⟩ | ↓🔲   Flames<br><br>T   TURN UP THE H....  *fx* ▲ |
| | To create a clipping mask from the type layer. The Layers panel indicates the clipped layer. |
| 3  Select the Flames layer | If necessary. |
| Resize the layer | (Use the Free Transform command.) So that it fills the text. |
| 4  Press ⟨SHIFT⟩ and click the TURN UP THE HEAT layer | (In the Layers panel.) To select both layers in the group so you can link them. |
| Click 🔗 | (The Link layers button.) To link the two layers. Any time you move the content of either of these layers, the contents of both layers will move together. |
| 5  Using the Move tool, drag the word **TURN** | To observe that the two layers move together. |
| Undo the move | Press Ctrl+Z. |
| 6  Update the image | |

## Layer filtering

*Explanation*

A Photoshop image can contain as many as 8,000 layers. While most of your images won't come close to having this many layers, using groups, links, and color coding can help manage multiple layers. You can also filter layers to search by different properties.

To filter layers, in the Layers panel, select an option from the drop-down list shown in Exhibit 1-3. Then choose a property (or enter a search term) in the options that appear at the right of the list. Photoshop will display only those layers that match the options you select. Once you've specified filtering options, you can click the red toggle button at the right of the Layers panel to turn filtering off; doing so will preserve the filtering options you've selected so that they'll be active again when you toggle filtering back on.

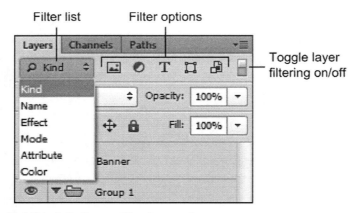

*Exhibit 1-3: Layer filtering options*

*Do it!*    **A-3:   Filtering layers**

| Here's how | Here's why |
|---|---|
| 1  In the Layers panel, click as shown | 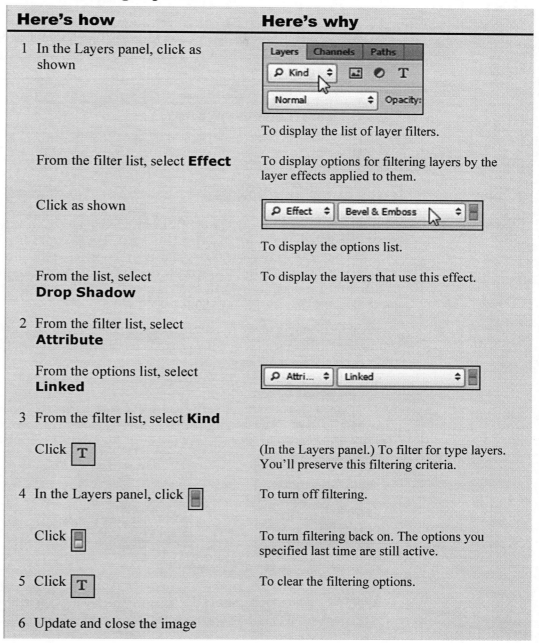 |
|  | To display the list of layer filters. |
| From the filter list, select **Effect** | To display options for filtering layers by the layer effects applied to them. |
| Click as shown |  |
|  | To display the options list. |
| From the list, select **Drop Shadow** | To display the layers that use this effect. |
| 2  From the filter list, select **Attribute** |  |
| From the options list, select **Linked** |  |
| 3  From the filter list, select **Kind** |  |
| Click T | (In the Layers panel.) To filter for type layers. You'll preserve this filtering criteria. |
| 4  In the Layers panel, click ▣ | To turn off filtering. |
| Click ▣ | To turn filtering back on. The options you specified last time are still active. |
| 5  Click T | To clear the filtering options. |
| 6  Update and close the image |  |

# Topic B: Blending modes

This topic covers the following ACE exam objectives for Photoshop CS6.

| # | Objective |
|---|-----------|
| **5.6** | **Understanding layer blend modes** |
| 5.6.1 | Toggling blend modes using keyboard shortcuts |
| 5.6.2 | Explanation of blend mode functions and usage |

## Layer blending modes

*Explanation*

You can create sophisticated layer effects by applying *blending modes*, which blend a layer into underlying layers in a variety of ways. For example, if you apply the Multiply blending mode to a layer, the pixels in that layer combine with pixels in layers below to darken where they overlap. If you apply the Screen blending mode to a layer, the pixels in that layer combine with pixels in layers below to lighten where they overlap. Both of these examples are shown in Exhibit 1-4.

Applying a blending mode is a *nondestructive effect*, meaning that it doesn't permanently alter the pixels in the image. You can remove a blending mode or apply a different blending mode at any time.

The horizontal bars are on a layer above the vertical bars, with the Normal blending mode applied

The same image, with the Multiply blending mode applied to the top layer

The same image, with the Screen blending mode applied to the top layer

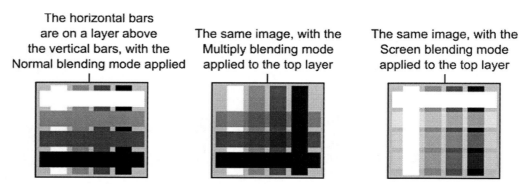

*Exhibit 1-4: Several examples of how layer blending modes affect image layers*

To apply a blending mode, select the layer to which you want to apply it. Then, in the Layers panel, from the Blending mode list, select a blending mode, as shown in Exhibit 1-5.

The modes in the Blending mode list are organized into groups, with similar modes grouped together. Because it can be difficult to anticipate exactly how a particular blending mode will affect an image, you might want to experiment by first selecting a blending mode that you think will give the results you want and then trying other modes in the same group. To quickly apply the next blending mode in the list, press Alt+Shift++ (Alt + Shift + plus sign). To move backward in the list, press Alt+Shift+− (Alt + Shift + minus sign). (Note that these keyboard shortcuts won't work if any option, including the Blending mode list, is selected in the Layers panel. Click in the image to deselect the Layers panel.)

*Exhibit 1-5: A blending mode selected in the Layers panel*

The following table describes each blending mode. The *blend color* is the pixel color in the layer to which you're applying the blending mode. The blend color mixes with the color below—the *base color*—to produce the *result color*.

| Blending mode | Description |
|---|---|
| Normal | Applies no blending effect. This is the default mode. |
| Dissolve | Randomly paints each pixel to create the result color. The result depends on the opacity at the pixel location. |
| Darken | Uses whichever color is darker: the blend color or the base color. |
| Multiply | Multiplies the blend color with the base color. The result is always a darker color than either of the original colors. |
| Color Burn | Darkens the base color to reflect the blend color by increasing the contrast. |
| Linear Burn | Darkens the base color by decreasing brightness. Similar to Color Burn, but the Linear Burn result is usually darker than the Color Burn result. |
| Darker Color | Displays the darkest values from the blend and base colors. |
| Lighten | Uses whichever color is lighter: the blend color or the base color. |
| Screen | Multiplies the inverse of the colors being blended. The result is always a lighter color than either of the original colors. Screening with a black color does not change the color beneath. Screening with white produces white, as shown in Exhibit 1-4. |
| Color Dodge | Brightens the base color to match the blend color by decreasing contrast. |

| Blending mode | Description |
| --- | --- |
| Linear Dodge (Add) | Brightens the base color to match the blend color by increasing brightness. The result of Linear Dodge is usually brighter than the result of Color Dodge. |
| Lighter color | Displays the lightest values from the blend and base colors. |
| Overlay | Multiplies or screens colors based on the base color. The highlights or shadows of the objects below show through, while mid-range colors and patterns are blended as with Multiply mode. |
| Soft Light | Darkens or lightens the image, depending on the color being blended. If the blend color is lighter than 50% gray, the image is lightened. If the blend color is darker than 50% gray, the image is darkened. The effect is to make the shadows and highlights more pronounced. |
| Hard Light | Similar to Soft Light but with a more pronounced effect, as if you're shining a bright spotlight. |
| Vivid Light | For blend colors lighter than 50% gray, lightens the image by increasing contrast. For darker blend colors, darkens the image by decreasing contrast. |
| Linear Light | Similar to Vivid Light, except that it lightens or darkens an image by increasing or decreasing brightness. |
| Pin Light | Replaces colors, depending on the blend color's brightness. For lighter blend colors, pixels darker than the blend color are replaced, and the lighter pixels don't change. For darker blend colors, the pixels lighter than the blend color are replaced, and the darker pixels don't change. |
| Hard Mix | Replaces colors to generate a posterized image consisting of up to eight colors. Generally, lighter colors lighten the result, and darker colors darken the result. |
| Difference | Subtracts the brighter color from the darker color. Blending with white inverts the base color. |
| Exclusion | Creates an effect similar to Difference but with less contrast. |
| Subtract | Based on the color information in each channel, subtracts the blend color from the base color. |
| Divide | Based on the color information in each channel, divides the blend color from the base color. |
| Hue | Creates an effect by using the luminance and saturation of the pixels below and the hue of the blend color. If the blend object is a solid color, the underlying image is colorized. |
| Saturation | Creates an effect by using the luminance and color of the pixels below and the saturation of the blend color. |
| Color | Creates an effect by using the luminance of the pixels below and the saturation and color of the blend color. If the blend object is a solid color, the underlying image is colorized, usually with a more pronounced effect than that produced by the Hue blending mode. |
| Luminosity | Creates an effect by using the saturation and color of the pixels below and the luminance of the blend color. |

**Duplicating layers**

One way to experiment with blending modes is to make a duplicate of a layer and apply blending modes to it. You can then adjust the layer stacking order to see how the duplicate layer affects the image. To duplicate a layer, use any of the following techniques:

- In the Layers panel, drag the layer onto the "Create a new layer" icon.
- From the Layers panel menu, choose Duplicate Layer. In the Duplicate Layer dialog box, enter a name for the duplicate layer, and click OK.
- With no pixels selected, choose Layer, New, Layer via Copy or press Ctrl+J.

*Do it!*

## B-1:    Applying layer blending modes

The files for this activity are in Student Data folder **Unit 1\Topic B**.

| Here's how | Here's why |
|---|---|
| 1 Open Hot peppers 2 | |
| Save the image as **My hot peppers 2** | (In the current topic folder.) You'll make the Alarm layer blend with the one below it. |
| 2 Hide the Clipping mask layer group | In the Layers panel, click the eye icon to the left of the layer group to hide all layers in the group. |
| 3 Select the **Peppers** layer | You'll try several blending modes to see how they blend the Peppers and Background layers. |
| Click in the image | To deselect the Layers panel. |
| 4 Press ( ALT ) + ( SHIFT ) + ( + ) | To select the Dissolve blending mode. Since this blending mode uses the opacity of the layer, you don't see any effect. |
| Press ( ALT ) + ( SHIFT ) + ( + ) | To select the Darken blending mode. This blending mode uses the dark colors from the Background layer. |
| 5 From the Blending mode list, select **Exclusion** | |
| Press ( ↑ ) | To select the previous blending mode in the list, Difference. |
| 6 Show the Clipping mask layer group | |
| 7 Select the **Clipping mask** layer group | You'll apply a blending mode to the layer group, which affects all layers in the group as if they were a single flattened layer. |
| From the Blending mode list, select **Linear Dodge (Add)** | |
| 8 Update and close the image | |

# Topic C: Smart Objects

*Explanation*

When applying transformations and other types of changes to layers, you can make those changes nondestructive by converting layers to Smart Objects. A Smart Object is an object that acts as a layer but stores the original image data of one or more layers. Smart Objects allow you to transform an image to smaller sizes and then back to the original size with no loss in quality.

## Nondestructive editing

Transforming image content, such as by rotating, scaling, or warping, is typically a destructive edit. A *destructive edit* is one that permanently changes pixel data. Therefore, transforming an image can degrade image quality. For example, if you scale a layer to 25% of its initial size, the layer content is rendered with fewer pixels. If you later scale the layer back to its original size, it will likely appear blurry.

You can transform image content nondestructively by converting it to a Smart Object. A Smart Object stores the original image data and references that data each time you apply a transformation. Therefore, you can transform a Smart Object, and each time, it's as though you're transforming the original image data, as shown in Exhibit 1-6.

Transformed layer content      Transformed Smart Object

Both items were scaled to 20% and then scaled back to their original size

*Exhibit 1-6: Transformed layer content compared to a transformed Smart Object*

### Converting layers to Smart Objects

You can convert one or more layers to a single Smart Object. In the Layers panel, a Smart Object looks like a layer, but its thumbnail has a Smart Object badge icon.

To convert to a Smart Object, select the layer or layers you want to convert and choose Convert to Smart Object from the Layers panel menu. The layers appear as a single Smart Object in the Layers panel, and the Smart Object badge appears on the thumbnail.

After converting a layer or layers to a Smart Object, you can transform the Smart Object without cumulatively degrading the image with each new transformation. For example, you can choose Edit, Free Transform to use the Free Transform command to resize objects proportionally.

*Do it!*

## C-1:   Creating and transforming Smart Objects

The files for this activity are in Student Data folder **Unit 1\Topic C**.

| Here's how | Here's why |
|---|---|
| 1  Open Postcard 1 | |
| Save the image as **My postcard 1** | (In the current topic folder.) You want to resize and arrange these layers, but you're not sure how. |
| 2  Select the **Pumpkin** layer | |
| Press CTRL + T | |
| Press SHIFT and scale the layer down to **20%** | Pressing Shift scales the selection proportionally. |
| Press ↵ ENTER | You decide this is too small. |
| 3  Using the Free Transform tool, scale the layer back up to match the other objects | The content of the layer is blurred. You'll restart the process and use Smart Objects. |
| 4  Choose **File**, **Revert** | |
| 5  From the Layers panel menu, choose **Convert to Smart Object** | |
| Observe the badge on the layer thumbnail | 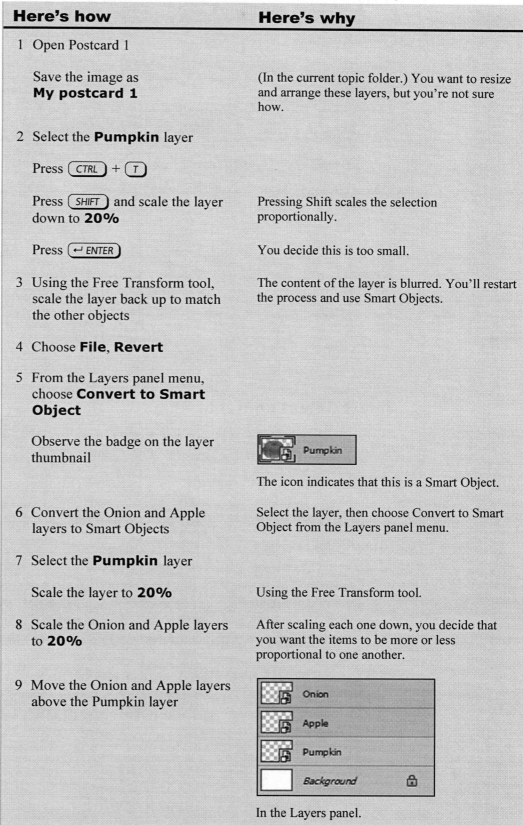 |
| | The icon indicates that this is a Smart Object. |
| 6  Convert the Onion and Apple layers to Smart Objects | Select the layer, then choose Convert to Smart Object from the Layers panel menu. |
| 7  Select the **Pumpkin** layer | |
| Scale the layer to **20%** | Using the Free Transform tool. |
| 8  Scale the Onion and Apple layers to **20%** | After scaling each one down, you decide that you want the items to be more or less proportional to one another. |
| 9  Move the Onion and Apple layers above the Pumpkin layer | |
| | In the Layers panel. |

10 Select the **Pumpkin** layer

Scale the layer to approximately **60%**

Because the layer was converted to a Smart Object before it was scaled, the original layer was never actually scaled down. Therefore, it can be scaled back up without image degradation.

11 Select the Apple layer

Scale it to approximately **30%**

12 Arrange the three objects approximately as shown

13 Update the image

## Smart Object contents

*Explanation*

After converting a layer to a Smart Object, you can still access and modify the original content. In addition, you can export the Smart Object content as a separate file.

### Modifying Smart Object contents

If you convert several layers into a single Smart Object, you can still access each original layer and make changes that will be reflected in the Smart Object.

To modify the original content:

1 In the Layers panel, select the Smart Object.
2 From the Layers panel menu, choose Edit Contents (or double-click the layer thumbnail). A message box appears, explaining that after changing the Smart Object's contents, you'll have to save them to update the Smart Object.
3 Click OK. The original content that you converted to a Smart Object appears in a new window.
4 Modify the content as needed, and then choose File, Save.
5 Close the window displaying the edited content to return to the original image window. This window now displays the updated Smart Object.

**Exporting Smart Object contents**

You might want to export Smart Object content as a separate file so you can use it in other images. To do so, right-click a Smart Object in the Layers panel and choose Export Contents from the shortcut menu. In the Save dialog box that opens, enter a name for the exported content, and click Save.

The image is exported as a Smart Object file, which uses the PSB file format. You can place the file in other image files as a Smart Object, or you can open it directly in its own image window.

*Do it!*

## C-2:   Working with Smart Object contents

| Here's how | Here's why |
|---|---|
| 1 Select the **Onion** layer | You decide that you like this arrangement and might want to use it in other images. You'll convert the layers into a single Smart Object to make them easier to work with and to preserve them from destructive transformations. |
| Press ( SHIFT ) and click the **Pumpkin** layer | To select all three Smart Object layers. |
| Right-click one of the selected layers and choose **Convert to Smart Object** | <br><br> To convert the layers into a single Smart Object. |
| Rename the layer **Fall harvest** | |
| 2 In the Layers panel, click [ *fx.* ] | The Add a layer style button. |
| Choose **Drop Shadow...** | To open the Layer Style dialog box. |
| Click **OK** | (To use the default settings.) The Drop Shadow is applied to the object as though it were a single layer. |
| 3 From the Layers panel menu, choose **Edit Contents** | A message box appears, stating that you must choose File, Save to commit your changes after editing the content. |
| Click **OK** | To open the Smart Object in a new tab. |
| Observe the Layers panel | The original Smart Objects you created are still there. |
| 4 Right-click the Onion layer and choose **Edit Contents** | |
| Click **OK** | To close the message box and open the Smart Object in a new tab. |

| | | |
|---|---|---|
| 5 | Select the **Apple** layer | |
| | Press ⬅ a few times | To nudge the layer to the left. |
| 6 | Press CTRL + S | |
| | Press CTRL + W | To return to My postcard 1. |
| 7 | Right-click the Fall harvest layer | |
| | Choose **Export Contents...** | To open the Save dialog box. Notice that the file type is PSB. A PSB file can be placed in other images as a Smart Object. |
| | Navigate to the current topic folder | Student Data folder Unit 1\Topic C. |
| | Edit the File name box to **Fall harvest** | |
| | Click **Save** | To export the object. |
| 8 | Update the image | |

### Vector Smart Objects

*Explanation*

Smart Objects can store vector data. If you place an Illustrator file into a Photoshop image, the file is placed as a Smart Object, maintaining the original vector data. Therefore, you can transform and manipulate the placed vector file without having to rasterize it. Because vector images can be scaled up without any loss of image quality or crispness, you can safely scale a vector Smart Object to larger than its original size.

To place a vector file into an image as a Smart Object:

1 Choose File, Place to open the Place dialog box.
2 Select the vector file and click Place. The Place PDF dialog box appears.
3 Click OK and press Enter to display the placed content as a Smart Object.

You can right-click a Smart Object based on an Illustrator file and choose Edit Contents to open the file in Adobe Illustrator, if you have that software on your computer.

*Do it!*

### C-3:    Placing and editing vector Smart Objects

The files for this activity are in Student Data folder **Unit 1\Topic C**.

| Here's how | Here's why |
|---|---|
| 1 Choose **File**, **Place...** | (To open the Place dialog box.) You'll place an Illustrator file in the image. |
| Select **Postcard art 1** | |
| Click **Place** | To open the Place PDF dialog box. |
| 2 From the Crop To list, select **Art Box** | |
| Click **OK** | To place the Illustrator file. |
| Press ⏎ ENTER | To commit the change. You could further transform this Smart Object without degrading the image quality. |
| 3 Move the Postcard art 1 layer below the Fall harvest layer | The Illustrator file contains some items you want to remove. |
| 4 Double-click the Postcard art 1 layer thumbnail | |
| Click **OK** | To close the dialog box and open the Smart Object in Illustrator. In Illustrator, a dialog box appears, asking if you want to discard or keep changes. |
| Click **OK** | |
| 5 Select the carrots | |
| Click DELETE | |

6  Update and close the file

7  In Photoshop, observe the image    The Smart Object reflects the changes you made.

8  Move and scale the Fall harvest layer

(If necessary.) To fit in the rectangle.

9  Update and close the image

# Topic D:   Layer comps

This topic covers the following ACE exam objectives for Photoshop CS6.

| # | Objective |
|---|-----------|
| **8.3** | **Working with layer comps** |
| 8.3.1 | Creating layer comps |
| 8.3.2 | Specifying what changes in a layer comp |
| 8.3.3 | Updating changes in layer comps |

## Comps as project deliverables

*Explanation*   When you're preparing an image that other people will review and approve, you'll probably want to create several versions of it. Multiple versions of a design or layout are typically called *comps*, which is short for *compositions*. You can use Photoshop to generate multiple comps in a single image file.

## The Layer Comps panel

You can use the Layer Comps panel to store comps of an image. Each layer comp is a snapshot of the Layers panel in a specified state. A layer comp stores three types of layer data for each layer:

- Layer visibility
- The position of layer content in the image
- The layer's appearance (style and blending mode)

If you have created layer groups for an image, each layer comp can contain some, all, or none of those layer groups.

### Creating layer comps

To create a layer comp:

1   Specify layer options for the appearance of the image in a given comp.
2   Choose Window, Layer Comps, or click the Layer Comps tab in the panel well, to open the Layer Comps panel.
3   At the bottom of the panel, click the Create New Layer Comp button to open the New Layer Comp dialog box.
4   Enter a name for the comp, specify the Layers panel settings you want the comp to use, and click OK.

### Viewing layer comps

To view your layer comps, click to the left of each layer comp's name in the Layer Comps panel, as shown in Exhibit 1-7. You can also click the Apply Next and Apply Previous buttons to cycle through the layer comps.

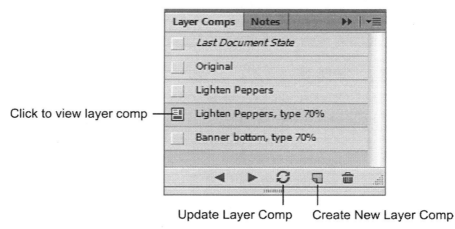

Click to view layer comp ——

Update Layer Comp    Create New Layer Comp

*Exhibit 1-7: The Layer Comps panel*

**Modifying layer comps**

Changes you make in an image while viewing a layer comp do not automatically update the layer comp itself. To modify a layer comp:

1    In the Layer Comps panel, select the layer comp you want to change.

2    Make your changes in the image.

3    In the Layer Comps panel, click the Update Layer Comp button.

*Do it!*    ## D-1: Creating layer comps

The files for this activity are in Student Data folder **Unit 1\Topic D**.

| Here's how | Here's why |
|---|---|
| 1  Open Hot peppers 3 | |
| Save the image as **My hot peppers 3** | In the current topic folder. |
| 2  Choose **Window, Layer Comps** | To open the Layer Comps panel. |
| 3  Click [ ] | (The Create New Layer Comp button.) To open the New Layer Comp dialog box. |
| Edit the Name box to read **Original** | |
| Check **Visibility**, **Position**, and **Appearance (Layer Style)** | |
| Click **OK** | To close the dialog box. |
| 4  Select the **Peppers** layer | |
| Apply the **Lighten** blending mode to the layer | |

5  Create a new layer comp called **Lighten Peppers**

In the Layer Comps panel, click the Create New Layer Comp button. Enter the comp name and click OK.

This layer comp preserves the settings currently specified.

6  Select the **Clipping mask** layer group

Set the Opacity to **70%**

7  Create a new layer comp named **Lighten Peppers, Type 70%**

8  Select the **Banner** layer

Drag the layer to the bottom edge of the image

9  Select the **Flames** layer

Drag the layer up

So that the type isn't covered by the banner.

10  Apply the **Normal** blending mode to the Peppers layer

11  Create a new layer comp named **Banner bottom, Type 70%**

12  In the Layer Comps panel, click the box to the left of the Lighten Peppers, type 70% layer comp

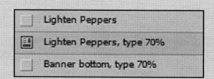

To view the comp.

13  Move the Flames layer down slightly in the image

In the Layer Comps panel, click [⟳]

(The Update Layer Comp icon.) To update the layer comp with the change.

14  Click the box next to each layer comp

To view them.

Close the Layer Comps panel

Update the image

Next, you'll make PDF files to give to a client, with each comp in a separate file.

## Exporting comps

*Explanation*  You can export layer comps as separate files. This capability is useful when you want to show the layer comps to a client. To export layer comps:

1 Choose File, Scripts, Layer Comps to Files.
2 Select a destination folder for the files.
3 Edit the file name prefix, if desired. The entire file name will consist of this prefix, followed by an incrementing four-digit number, followed by the name of the layer comp as it is listed in the Layer Comps panel.
4 From the File Type list, select a file type, such as PDF.
5 Click Run. When the script finishes, click OK.

*Do it!*  ### D-2: Exporting layer comps

| Here's how | Here's why |
|---|---|
| 1 Choose **File, Scripts, Layer Comps to PDF...** | To open the Layer Comps To PDF dialog box. |
| Click **Browse** | To open the Choose Folder dialog box. |
| Navigate to the current topic folder | Student Data folder Unit 1\Topic D. |
| In the File name box, enter **My layer comp** | |
| Click **Save** | To return to the Layer Comps To Files dialog box. |
| 2 Click **Run** | When the conversion process is finished, the Script Alert dialog box appears. |
| Click **OK** | |
| 3 In Windows Explorer, navigate to the current topic folder | |
| Open My layer comps | A warning box appears, indicating that Adobe Reader is attempting to switch to full screen mode. |
| Click **Yes** | To view the slideshow. |
| 4 Close Adobe Reader | |
| 5 Update and close the image | In Photoshop. |

# Unit summary: Working with multiple layers

*Topic A*    In this topic, you learned how to create **layer groups**. Then you applied a **clipping mask** to a layer to control visibility. You also learned how to **filter** layers.

*Topic B*    In this topic, you applied **blending modes** to layers to change how their pixels interact with those of other layers.

*Topic C*    In this topic, you converted layers to **Smart Objects** and transformed them. You also modified the contents of Smart Objects and exported them. Finally, you placed a vector file as a Smart Object.

*Topic D*    In this topic, you used the Layer Comps panel to create **layer comps**. You also viewed and modified layer comps. Finally, you exported layer comps.

## Review questions

1  How can you specify that the contents of several layers always move as a unit, without flattening the layers? [Choose all that apply.]

A  Select each of the layers, and from the Layers panel menu, choose Merge Layers.

B  Select each of the layers, and choose Layers, Smart Objects, Group into New Smart Object.

C  Select each of the layers, and from the Layers panel menu, choose Link Layers.

D  Select each of the layers, and click the Link layers button in the Layers panel.

2  To organize layers so they appear in a collapsible layer with a folder icon, you should:

A  Link them.

B  Group them.

C  Create a clipping mask.

D  Combine them into a Smart Object.

3  You want to filter layers to find those that use the Lighten blending mode. Then you want to preserve the filter settings to use later as you work in the image. How would you do this?

4  True or false? Applying a blend mode is a destructive edit.

5  Which of the following statements are true of Smart Objects? [Choose all that apply.]

A  A Smart Object can be transformed to a small size and then back to its original size with no loss of quality.

B  A Smart Object's data cannot be edited after you've converted it from layer data.

C  Only raster, not vector, data can be stored as a Smart Object.

D  You can combine multiple layers into one Smart Object.

6 How can you convert several selected layers into a Smart Object?

  A From the Layers panel menu, choose New Group.

  B From the Layers panel menu, choose Convert to Smart Object.

  C From the Layers panel menu, choose New Group from Layers.

  D From the Layers panel menu, choose Merge Layers.

7 Which types of layer data can vary among layer comps for a single layer? [Choose all that apply.]

  A Layer visibility

  B Pixel content

  C The position of layer content in the image

  D The layer blending mode

8 From which submenu can you export layer comps?

  A File, Automate

  B File, Scripts

  C File, Export

  D File, Place

## Independent practice activity

In this activity, you'll group layers and filter them to find specific attributes. You'll also apply blending modes and create Smart Objects. Finally, you'll create layer comps.

The files for this activity are in Student Data folder **Unit 1\Unit summary**.

1 Open Turn up the heat 1 and save it as **My turn up the heat 1**.

2 Place the file Market banner in the image at the top of the layer stacking order.

3 Move the Market banner layer to the top edge of the image.

4 Create a layer group from the layers "turn up the" and "HEAT."

5 Convert the Flames layer to a Smart Object.

6 Move the Flames layer above the HEAT layer. (*Hint*: The HEAT layer is in the layer group you created.)

7 Clip the Flames layer to the HEAT layer.

8 Rotate the Flames layer 90 degrees counterclockwise. Then scale it vertically so that it fits the image height, and position it so that it shows through the HEAT layer, as shown in Exhibit 1-8.

9 Apply the Overlay blending mode to the layer group you created.

10 Create a new layer comp named Overlay.

11 Apply the Pin Light blending mode to the Alarm layer.

12 Create a new layer comp named Overlay, Pin Light.

13 View each layer comp.

14  Search for layers that have Smart Objects. Then remove the search filter. (*Hint*: use the Kind category to filter the layers, then select the appropriate filter option. Click the option again to remove it.)

15  Update and close the image.

*Exhibit 1-8: The My turn up the heat 1 image as it appears after Step 8*

# Unit 2

## Working with color

Complete this unit, and you'll know how to:

**A** Specify colors and store them in the Swatches panel, and apply colors to image selections and as fill layers.

**B** Apply fill types such as gradients, and use overlay layer styles to apply colors and gradients to layer content.

**C** Select color in an image, adjust color, colorize an image, create a spot-color channel, and replace a color in an image.

# Topic A:   Filling image areas

*Explanation*

As you create and modify images and artwork, you can apply color to selected image areas. To specify a color, you can use the Color panel, the Swatches panel, the Color Picker dialog box, or the Eyedropper tool.

## The Swatches panel

If you're using the same colors repeatedly, you should save them as swatches in the Swatches panel so you won't need to redefine or resample them each time you want to use them. The Swatches panel displays a set of *swatches* (colors) as small color squares by default. You can select a different set of swatches—such as Pantone colors or Web-safe colors—from the Swatches panel menu. In addition, you can customize the Swatches panel by adding your own colors. You can also change how the swatches are displayed in the panel. For example, you can choose Small List from the Swatches panel menu to display the swatches with their names as a list, as shown in Exhibit 2-1.

To add a color to the Swatches panel:

1   Specify the foreground color by using the Color panel, the Eyedropper tool, or the Color Picker dialog box.

2   Add the color to the Swatches panel by using either of these techniques:

• Point to an empty area at the bottom of the Swatches panel, so the pointer appears as a paint bucket, and click to add the color. In the Color Swatch Name dialog box that appears, enter a name and click OK.

• Click the "Create new swatch of foreground color" button to open the Color Swatch Name dialog box. Enter a name and click OK.

To remove a swatch from the Swatches panel, drag the swatch to the Delete swatch icon, or press Alt and click the swatch.

Create a new swatch
of foreground color

*Exhibit 2-1: The Swatches panel in Small List view*

## HSB color

You can use the Color panel to specify colors by using a variety of color models, such as RGB, CMYK, or grayscale. Some people prefer to define color by using the *HSB* (hue, saturation, brightness) color model, which many find to be more intuitive. The HSB color model's range is similar to RGB's, but HSB defines colors based on their hue, saturation, and brightness, as shown in Exhibit 2-2.

The hue value is measured in degrees, based on the concept of all available hues being displayed on a circle known as a color wheel. Each degree in the circle represents a different hue along a spectrum. The saturation and brightness values are measured in percentages.

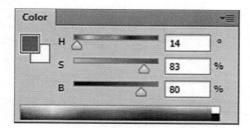

*Exhibit 2-2: The Color panel displaying the HSB color sliders*

*Do it!*

## A-1: Creating swatches

The files for this activity are in Student Data folder **Unit 2\Topic A**.

| Here's how | Here's why |
|---|---|
| 1 Open Market logo 1 | |
| Save the image as **My market logo 1** | In the current topic folder. |
| 2 Press (CTRL) + (1) | (If necessary.) To zoom to Actual Pixels. |
| Select the Eyedropper tool | |
| Click inside the **M** | To sample the orange color as the new foreground color. |

3  Click the **Swatches** panel

Point to the blank area just to the right of the last swatch, as shown

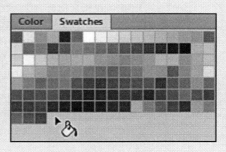

The pointer changes to a paint can.

Click the mouse button

To add the foreground color as a swatch. The Color Swatch Name dialog box appears.

Edit the Name box to read **Harvest Valley orange**

Click **OK**

To add the orange color to the Swatches panel.

4  From the Swatches panel, menu, choose **Small List**

To display the swatches as a list.

Scroll to the bottom of the list

To view the Harvest Valley orange swatch.

5  Drag the Swatches panel tab to the left

To separate the panel from its panel group so you can see the Swatches and Color panels at the same time.

Drag the Swatches panel next to the Color panel group, as shown

6  From the Color panel menu, choose **HSB Sliders**

To display the HSB color model's sliders. You'll use this color model to specify a slightly dimmer version of the color.

Drag the B (Brightness) slider to **80**

To specify a dimmer color.

7  In the Swatches panel, click [⬐]    (The "Create new swatch of foreground color" button.) To open the Color Swatch Name dialog box.

   Edit the Name box to read **Darker HV orange**

   Click **OK**    To add the adjusted color as a new swatch. Next, you'll create a lighter version of the color.

8  In the Color panel, drag the B slider to **100**

   Drag the S (Saturation) slider to **60**    To create a pale orange.

9  In the Swatches panel, click [⬐]

   Edit the Name box to read **Lighter HV orange**

   Click **OK**

10 Create a color named **Very light HV orange**, with a Saturation value of **40**    In the Color panel, drag the S slider to 40. In the Swatches panel, click the "Create new swatch of foreground color" button. Enter "Very light HV orange" and click OK.

11 In the Swatches panel, click **Darker HV orange**    To select it as the foreground color

   Press (CTRL) and click **Hidden Valley orange**    To select it as the background color.

   Press (ALT) and click **Very light HV orange**    To delete the swatch.

12 Reset the workspace    From the Workspace list, select Reset Essentials.

   Close the image

### Fill shortcuts

*Explanation*

After you set a color as the foreground or background color, you can apply it by using a variety of techniques.

- To fill a selection on the Background layer with the background color, press Backspace or Delete. (On other layers, pressing Backspace or Delete removes pixels, creating empty areas.)
- To fill a selection with the foreground color, press Alt+Backspace or Alt+Delete.
- To fill a selection with the background color, press Ctrl+Backspace or Ctrl+Delete.
- To apply a fill with custom settings, choose Edit, Fill or press Shift+Backspace to open the Fill dialog box. From the Use list, select Foreground Color or Background Color, or select Color to open the Color Picker, from which you can select any color to use as the new fill. Under Blending, select a mode and specify the opacity for the color you're applying, as shown in Exhibit 2-3.

When you use the Fill dialog box to specify a blending mode for the fill you're applying, the blending mode influences how the new fill affects the existing colors on the current layer. The blending mode won't affect how the new fill interacts with colors on other layers.

*Exhibit 2-3: The Fill dialog box*

# File presets

When you choose File, New to create a Photoshop file, you can specify the image's size, resolution, color mode, and background color. Rather than specifying each value manually, you can select an option from the Preset list to specify a standard size or other preset. The following table lists a few of the presets available.

| Preset | Specifications |
|---|---|
| Clipboard | Uses the dimensions and resolution of the item currently on the Clipboard. This is useful when you've cut or copied content that you want to paste into a new Photoshop file. |
| Default Photoshop Size | 7" × 5" at 72ppi. |
| U.S. Paper | 8.5" × 11" at 300 ppi. |
| International Paper | 210 mm × 297 mm at 300 ppi. |
| Photo | 3" × 2" at 300 ppi. |
| Web | 800 pixels × 600 pixels at 72 ppi. |
| Mobile & Devices | 240 pixels × 320 pixels at 72 ppi. |
| Film & Video | 720 pixels × 480 pixels at 72 ppi, with a pixel aspect ratio of 0.91. This matches the frame size of the NTSC video traditionally used for TV broadcasts in the United States. (There's also a widescreen setting with a pixel aspect ratio of 1.21.) |
| <open image name> | Any open images are listed at the bottom of the Preset list. You can select an image name to use its settings for the new image. |

*Do it!*

## A-2: Filling selections

| Here's how | Here's why |
|---|---|
| 1 Choose **File, New...** | To open the New dialog box. |
| Edit the Name box to read **My background 1** | |
| 2 From the Preset list, select **Default Photoshop Size** | If necessary. |
| 3 From the Width list, select **picas** | Width: 42 · Picas ▾ / Height: 30 · Picas ▾ |
| | To set both the width and the height to picas, a common measurement unit in print publishing. |
| Edit the Width and Height boxes to read **48** | |
| Edit the Resolution box to read **300** | |
| From the Color Mode list, select **CMYK Color** | Width: 48 · Picas ▾ / Height: 48 · Picas ▾ / Resolution: 300 · Pixels/Inch ▾ / Color Mode: CMYK Color ▾ · 8 bit ▾ |
| 4 Observe the Preset value | Because you specified custom settings, the Preset value automatically changed to "Custom." |
| Click **OK** | To create the new image. |
| 5 Press `CTRL` + `← BACKSPACE` | To fill the image with the current background color. |
| 6 Create a layer named **Circles** | Press Alt and click the "Create a new layer" button in the Layers panel. Enter "Circles" in the Name box, and click OK. |
| Create a circular selection | Use the Elliptical Marquee tool while pressing Shift to create a perfect circle. |
| 7 In the Swatches panel, click **Lighter HV orange** | To set the foreground color to Lighter orange. |
| Press `ALT` + `← BACKSPACE` | To fill the selection marquee with the foreground color. |
| Deselect the current selection | Press Ctrl+D. |

8  Make a smaller circular selection
   inside the first circle, as shown

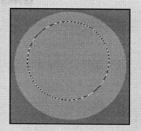

   Press ( ← BACKSPACE )                To delete the selected pixels from the Circles
                                        layer. Pressing Backspace removes the pixels
                                        and creates a transparent area within the
                                        selection.

   Hide, and then show, the             (In the Layers panel, click the eye icon next to
   Background layer                     the Background layer.) To view the transparent
                                        space.

9  Press ( CTRL ) and click            (In the Swatches panel.) To set that color as the
   **Darker HV orange**                background color.

10 Select the Circles layer            If necessary.

   Press ( CTRL ) + ( ← BACKSPACE )    To fill the selection with the background color.

   Deselect the current selection

11 On the Circles layer, draw an
   overlapping circular marquee, as
   shown

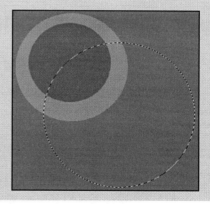

12 Verify that Lighter HV orange is
the current foreground color

Press (SHIFT) + (← BACKSPACE)

To open the Fill dialog box. You'll use a
blending mode to create a semi-transparent
effect.

From the Use list, select
**Foreground Color**

(If necessary.) To select the Lighter orange
color.

From the Mode list, select
**Screen**

To make the fill color lighten the colors it
overlaps.

Click **OK**

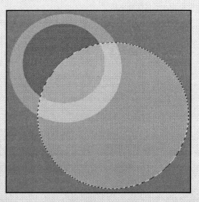

To fill the circle. The blending mode lightened
the two circles where the new circle overlaps
them.

13 Deselect the current selection

14 Create another circular selection,
as shown

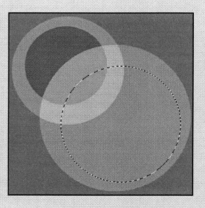

15 Open the Fill dialog box

Press Shift+Backspace.

From the Mode list, select
**Multiply**

Click **OK**

To fill the circle with the foreground color,
using the specified blending mode.

16  Deselect the current selection

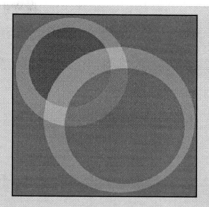

17  Press ⎡CTRL⎤ + ⎡S⎤                    To open the Save As dialog box. The name you
                                           specified when you created the image appears in
                                           the File name box.

     Navigate to the current topic
     folder and click **Save**

### Fill layers

*Explanation*

Another way to add a color to an image is to create a *fill layer*. A fill layer can contain a solid color, a gradient, or a pattern.

Applying a fill by using a fill layer requires fewer steps than does creating a blank layer and then filling it. In addition, you might want to use a fill layer to apply a solid color, a gradient, or a pattern because if you later change the image's canvas size, the fill layer will expand to fill the new space.

To create a fill layer:

1 Open the dialog box for the type of fill layer you want to create:

- At the bottom of the Layers panel, click the "Create new fill or adjustment layer" icon and choose Solid Color, Gradient, or Pattern to open the appropriate dialog box.
- Choose Layer, New Fill Layer and choose Solid Color, Gradient, or Pattern to open the New Layer dialog box. Specify the layer name and click OK to open the appropriate dialog box for the type of fill layer you chose.

2 Specify the settings you want.

3 Click OK.

Another benefit of using a fill layer is that you can easily change its settings by double-clicking the fill layer's thumbnail, shown in Exhibit 2-4, to open a dialog box in which you can adjust the color, gradient, or pattern of the fill layer.

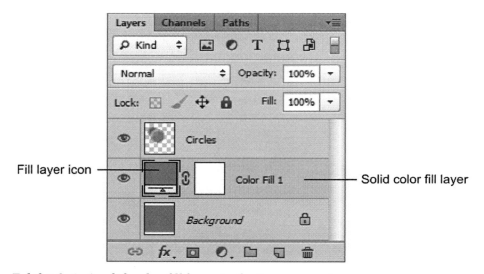

*Exhibit 2-4: A solid-color fill layer in the Layers panel*

*Do it!*   **A-3:   Creating fill layers**

| Here's how | Here's why |
|---|---|
| 1  Press D | To return the foreground and background colors to their defaults. |
| 2  Choose **Image, Canvas Size...** | To open the Canvas Size dialog box. You'll add one inch to the height of the canvas. |
| Edit the Height box to read **9** | |
| Verify that Relative is cleared | |
| In the Canvas extension color list, verify that **Background** is selected | |
| Click **OK** | The canvas extends an additional inch, but the additional canvas is white (the current background color). |
| 3  Press CTRL + Z | To undo the change. You'll create a fill layer with the background color to see what happens when you resize the canvas. |
| 4  In the Layers panel, click ⊘▾ | The "Create new fill or adjustment layer" icon. |
| Choose **Solid color...** | To open the Color Picker (Solid color) dialog box. |
| In the Swatches panel, click **Harvest Valley orange** | |
| Click **OK** | |
| 5  Drag the **Color Fill 1** layer below the Circles layer | (In the Layers panel.) You'll add to the canvas size to see the result of the fill layer. |
| 6  Choose **Image, Canvas Size...** | To open the Canvas Size dialog box. |
| Edit the Height box to read **9** | |
| Click **OK** | The fill layer expands automatically as the canvas expands. |
| 7  Update and close the image | |

# Topic B: Gradients and overlays

*Explanation*

A *gradient* is a blend of two or more colors, in which the colors fade gradually from one to another. You can use the Gradient tool to drag within a layer or selection to specify the angle and length of a gradient. Another way to apply a fill, gradient, or pattern to a layer is to use an overlay layer style. An *overlay layer style* applies a fill, gradient, or pattern to only the existing pixels in a layer, similar to creating a layer clipping mask.

## The Gradient tool

To create a gradient with the Gradient tool:

1 In the Tools panel, select the Gradient tool.

2 On the options bar, open the Gradient Picker, shown in Exhibit 2-5. Select the gradient you want, or choose New Gradient from the Gradient Picker menu to create a custom gradient.

3 On the options bar, click the icon for the gradient type you want to use: Linear, Radial, Angle, Reflected, or Diamond.

The gradient type determines how the colors are arranged. For example, a linear gradient displays colors blending from one to another in a straight line. A radial gradient displays one color at the center and blends outward to the other colors.

4 Drag across the image or selection to specify the angle and length of the gradient.

The distance you drag the Gradient tool specifies the gradient's *blend area:* where the colors blend together. If you drag across only part of the layer or selection, the area outside that region is filled with the gradient's beginning or ending colors.

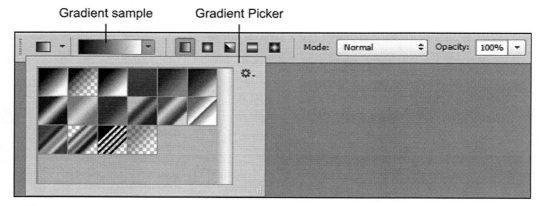

*Exhibit 2-5: Gradient tool options*

To modify the gradient's colors and other settings, click the gradient sample on the options bar to open the Gradient Editor dialog box, shown in Exhibit 2-6. To create a new gradient preset, enter a name and click New. Click OK when you're done editing the gradient.

The following table describes some of the settings in the Gradient Editor dialog box.

| Setting | Description |
|---|---|
| Panel menu | Choose a different set of gradients, or change how the gradient list is displayed. |
| Presets | Click a gradient to view and change its settings. When you do, its name changes to "Custom" so that your changes don't affect the original gradient. |
| Name box | Enter a name for the gradient. |
| Color stop | Click a color stop to select it so you can change its color. To move a color stop, drag it or type a position in the Location box. To add a color stop, click below the gradient bar. To remove a color stop, drag it away from the gradient bar. (A gradient must have at least two color stops, so you can't remove the last two.) |
| Opacity stop | Click an opacity stop to select it so you can change the opacity setting at that location. To move an opacity stop, drag it or type a new position in the Location box. Add an opacity stop by clicking above the gradient bar. Remove a stop by dragging it away from the gradient bar. |
| Midpoint | When you click a color stop or opacity stop, a diamond appears between it and the next stop. The diamond represents the blending midpoint between the two stops. To adjust the midpoint, drag it or type a new value in the Location box. |

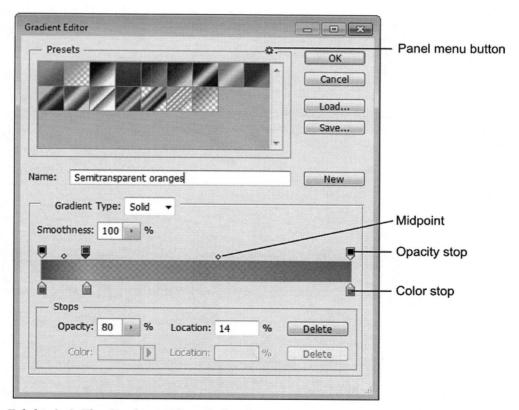

*Exhibit 2-6: The Gradient Editor dialog box*

## Gradient fill layers

You can apply a gradient to an entire layer by creating a gradient fill layer. To create a gradient fill layer:

1  In the Layers panel, click the "Create new fill or adjustment layer" icon and choose Gradient to open the Gradient Fill dialog box.

2  Specify the options you want.

3  Click OK.

To modify the gradient fill layer, double-click its icon in the Layers panel. In the Gradient Fill dialog box, specify the settings you want and click OK.

### Gradient Map adjustment

Another way to make use of gradients is to use the Gradient Map adjustment. This adjustment maps the colors of a specified gradient fill to the equivalent shadows, midtones, and highlights in an image. So, for example, if you mapped a three-color gradient fill to an image, one endpoint of the gradient would map to the shadows, the center color stop would map to the midtones, and the other endpoint would map to the highlights in the image. The result isn't a gradient (unless you've manually applied one in the image) but is rather an adjustment layer that replaces image colors.

To use the Gradient Map adjustment, click the Gradient Map icon in the Adjustments panel to create an adjustment layer. Then, in the Properties panel, select the desired gradient.

*Do it!*

## B-1:   Creating gradients

The files for this activity are in Student Data folder **Unit 2\Topic B**.

| Here's how | Here's why |
|---|---|
| 1  Open Background 2 | |
| Save the image as **My background 2** | In the current topic folder. |
| Press (CTRL) + (O) | To fit the image on the screen. |
| 2  Select the Circles layer | (If necessary.) In the Layers panel. |
| 3  Set the foreground color to **Lighter HV orange** | In the Swatches panel, click Lighter HV orange. |
| Set the background color to **Darker HV orange** | In the Swatches panel, press Ctrl and click Darker HV orange. |
| 4  Create a layer named **Fade** | |
| Drag the layer below the Circles layer | |
| 5  In the Tools panel, click | The Gradient tool. |
| Display the Gradient Picker | Click the Gradient Picker arrow on the options bar. |
| In the Gradient Picker, verify that the first gradient is selected, as shown | The Foreground to Background gradient. |
| Press (ESC) | To close the Gradient Picker. |
| 6  Drag from the top-left corner of the image to the bottom-right corner | To create the gradient. |
| Observe the image | The gradient goes from the top-left corner to the bottom-right corner. Next, you'll create a gradient and apply it to another layer. |
| 7  On the options bar, click the gradient sample | To open the Gradient Editor dialog box. You'll create a gradient that includes three colors. |

8 Click the left color stop, as shown

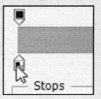

In the Swatches panel, click **Darker HV orange**

To apply the color as the foreground color of the gradient.

9 Click the right color stop, as shown

Set the color to **Harvest Valley orange**

In the Swatches panel, click Harvest Valley orange.

10 Click below the gradient bar, as shown

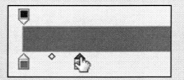

To create another color stop.

Set the color for the new stop to **Lighter HV orange**

Drag the color midpoint diamonds closer to the center color stop, as shown

To make the Lighter orange portion of the gradient narrower.

Next, you'll lower the opacity for the gradient at the center stop.

11 Click above the gradient bar, as shown

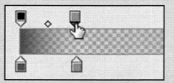

To create an opacity stop above the center color stop.

Under Stops, edit the Opacity value to read **80**

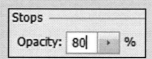

To create a slightly transparent area of the gradient.

12  Edit the Name box to read
    **Semitransparent oranges**

    Click **New**                              To save the custom gradient as a preset.

    Click **OK**                               To close the dialog box.

13  Above the Circles layer, create a
    layer named **Highlight**

    In the Highlight layer, use the            Drag from the top-right corner to the bottom-left
    **Semitransparent oranges**                corner. Because the new gradient is
    gradient to create a linear gradient       semitransparent, you can see through it to the
    extending from the top-right               circles you created on the layer below.
    corner of the image to the bottom-
    left corner

    Adjust the layer's Opacity to
    **30%**

14  Update and close the image

## Gradient overlays

*Explanation*

The Gradient Overlay layer style fills the existing layer content with the gradient you specify. This layer style is particularly useful for applying a gradient to text; even after applying a gradient overlay, you can continue to edit and format the text.

By default, a gradient overlay aligns with the layer content. Therefore, if you change the text on a type layer, or paint additional areas on a layer, the gradient adjusts automatically to flow across the new layer content.

To specify settings for the gradient overlay, select Gradient Overlay from the list of styles in the Layer Style dialog box. The Gradient Overlay style options are shown in Exhibit 2-7.

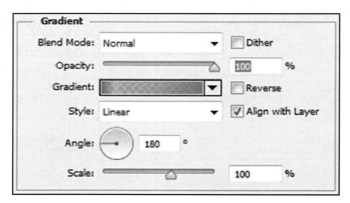

*Exhibit 2-7: The Gradient Overlay options in the Layer Style dialog box*

To create an overlay layer style:

1  Double-click the layer thumbnail or the space to the right of the layer name to open the Layer Style dialog box.

2  In the list of styles, select the type of overlay you want to use: Color Overlay, Gradient Overlay, or Pattern Overlay.

3  Specify the options you want to use, such as transparency.

4  For gradient and pattern overlays, point to the image and drag to reposition the gradient or pattern relative to the layer content through which it appears. This technique works only while the Layer Style dialog box is open.

5  Click OK.

*Do it!*

## B-2:   Filling areas with overlay layer styles

The files for this activity are in Student Data folder **Unit 2\Topic B**.

| Here's how | Here's why |
|---|---|
| 1  Open Background 3 | |
| Save the image as **My background 3** | In the current topic folder. |
| 2  Double-click the Fruit layer thumbnail | To open the Layer Style dialog box. You'll dim the nectarines to make them more subdued. |
| 3  Under Styles, click **Color Overlay** | (Click the words themselves, not the checkbox to their left). To check the checkbox and display the Color Overlay settings. |
| Click the color swatch next to the Blend Mode list, as shown | Blend Mode: Normal  Opacity: 100 %  To open the Color Picker (Overlay Color) dialog box. |
| Click as shown | To specify a black color. |

|  |  |
|---|---|
| R:  0 | C:  75  % |
| G:  0 | M:  68  % |
| B:  0 | Y:  67  % |
| #  000000 | K:  90  % |

| | |
|---|---|
| Click **OK** | To close the Color Picker (Overlay Color) dialog box. |
| Set the Opacity to **50%** | |
| Click **OK** | To overlay the layer with a semi-transparent black color, dimming it slightly. |
| 4  In the Layers panel, double-click the NECTARINES layer | To open the Layer Style dialog box. |

| | |
|---|---|
| 5 Click **Gradient Overlay** | To display the Gradient Overlay settings. |
| Display the Gradient Picker | In the Layer Style dialog box. |
| Select the **Semitransparent oranges** gradient, as indicated |  |
| Click **OK** | To close the Gradient Picker. |
| Set the Angle to **180** | To reverse the gradient colors. |
| Clear **Align with Layer** | |
| Click **OK** | To apply the gradient overlay to the type layer. |
| 6 Using the Move tool, drag the text to the left of the image | The colors in the text change as you move it. Because you cleared Align with Layer, the gradient applies to the whole image. |
| 7 In the NECTARINES layer, double-click the **Gradient Overlay** layer effect name | 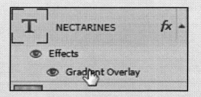 |
| | To open the Layer Style dialog box. |
| Check **Align with Layer** | |
| Click **OK** | To close the dialog box. |
| 8 Drag the text back to the right edge of the image | This time, the gradient "sticks" to the layer. |
| 9 Update and close the image | |

# Topic C:  Color adjustments

This topic covers the following ACE exam objectives for Photoshop CS6.

| # | Objective |
|---|-----------|
| **6.1** | **Differentiating between adjustment types** |
| 6.1.1 | Identifying the strengths and weaknesses of specific adjustments |
| 6.1.2 | Applying adjustment layers for dramatic effect or color correction |
| 6.1.3 | Blending adjustment types |
| **7.9** | **Selecting color** |
| 7.9.1 | Best practices for selecting color in an image and working with the appropriate color adjustment tools to isolate color casts for removal |
| 7.9.2 | Creating single color images and spot color designs |

## Color-based selections

*Explanation*

You can use the Magic Wand tool to select areas based on the similarity of pixel color and brightness. All pixels in an 8-bit image are assigned brightness values from 0 to 255, with 255 being the brightest. In a grayscale image, each pixel has one value between 0 and 255. But in a color image, each pixel can have several brightness values—one for each component color used by that pixel. For example, each pixel in an RGB (red, green, blue) image has three brightness values: one each for the red, green, and blue components. When you click a pixel with the Magic Wand tool, you select that pixel, along with other pixels within a specific range of color and brightness values.

### Magic Wand tolerance

You specify the range for the Magic Wand tool by entering a value in the Tolerance box on the options bar, shown in Exhibit 2-8. The higher the Tolerance value, the wider the range of pixels you will select. For example, if you set the Tolerance to 10, you can click a pixel to select all pixels with matching color and brightness values, as well as all pixels whose values range from 10 levels lower to 10 levels higher.

By default, the Magic Wand tool selects only pixels surrounding the one you clicked. If you want to select all image pixels within the specified tolerance range, clear the Contiguous check box on the options bar. To base the selection on all layers in an image, check Sample All Layers.

*Exhibit 2-8: Some options for the Magic Wand tool*

*Do it!*

### C-1:   Selecting with the Magic Wand tool

The files for this activity are in Student Data folder **Unit 2\Topic C**.

| Here's how | Here's why |
|---|---|
| 1  Open Planter 1 | |
| Save the image as **My planter 1** | In the current topic folder. |
| 2  Select the **Magic Wand Tool** | Right-click the Quick Selection tool and choose the Magic Wand tool. |
| 3  Click the top of the flower, as shown | |

To select a region of color within the default guidelines specified on the options bar.

Deselect the selected area

4  On the options bar, change the Tolerance value to **75**    To increase the tolerance for the Magic Wand tool so that more of the image will be selected.

Click the top of the flower again

This time, most of the color is selected.

Deselect the selected area

5  On the options bar, clear **Contiguous**    To select all areas in the image that match the sample you select, regardless of whether they're next to one another.

Click the top of the flower again    This time, several other areas with a similar color at the top-left of the image are selected, in addition to the flower.

Deselect the selected area

6  Update the image

## The Color Range command

*Explanation*

You can select a color or a range of colors by using the Color Range command. This command can be used to modify the color or tonal values of the selection or to replace the colors in the selection. Color Range can also be used to modify existing selections or layers to refine or narrow the selected colors or edges. The Color Range dialog box is shown in Exhibit 2-9.

To select a color range:

1   Choose Select, Color Range.

2   From the Select list, choose one of the following options:

- Sampled Colors — You can use an eyedropper to sample a color in the image. Other eyedroppers allow you to add to or subtract from the sample.

- A color range — Reds, Yellows, Greens, Cyans, Blues, or Magentas. This selection cannot be adjusted.

- A tonal range — Highlights, Midtones, or Shadows. This selection cannot be adjusted.

- Out-Of-Gamut

3   Adjust the fuzziness. The Fuzziness value determines the range of colors that are selected beyond the color you sampled. A higher value will include a broader range of colors.

4   If you want to exclude colors that are in range but farther from the selection point, check the Localized Color Clusters box. Use the Range box to set the size of the selected area.

5   Choose a preview option:

- Selection — Shows the parts of the image included in the selection. Areas not included will be black.

- Image — Shows the full image file. This is helpful if you are viewing only a portion of the image in the image window.

6   From the Selection Preview list, select an option. These previews will be displayed in the image window. The default is None. Other options are:

- Grayscale — Indicates the selection range in shades of gray. This is the same as the preview display.

- Black Matte — Displays color components of areas included within the selection range. Excluded areas are black.

- White Matte — Displays color components of areas included within the selection range. Excluded areas are white. For some images, this may be an easier way to see what is being included in the selection.

- Quick Mask — Applies a transparent red mask over the excluded areas, allowing you to see details in those areas.

7   If you want to change the selection range to the opposite colors of the currently selected range, check Invert.

8   Click OK to apply the selection.

You can also save and retrieve selection criteria by using the Save and Load buttons.

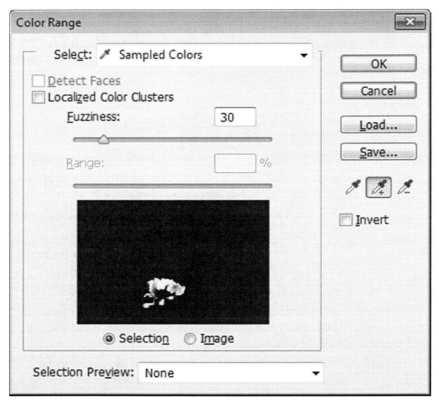

Exhibit 2-9: The Color Range dialog box

*Do it!*

## C-2: Selecting with the Color Range command

| Here's how | Here's why |
|---|---|
| 1 Choose **Select,** **Color Range...** | You'll select the red colors in the image to modify them without affecting the rest of the image. |
| 2 From the Select list, choose **Reds** | |
| Observe the preview | 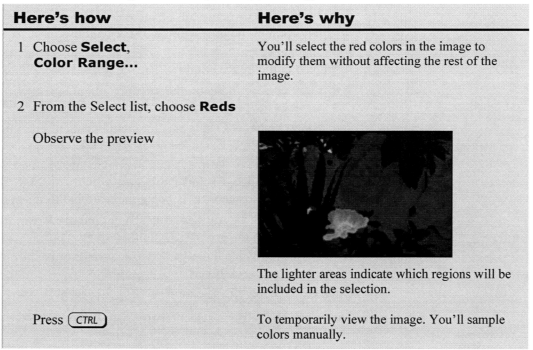 |
| | The lighter areas indicate which regions will be included in the selection. |
| Press (CTRL) | To temporarily view the image. You'll sample colors manually. |

3  From the Select list, choose                To activate the eyedropper tool.
   **Sampled Colors**

4  Click in the image as shown

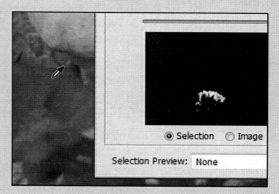

To select the color.

5  Select the **Add to Sample**
   eyedropper, as shown

You'll select another color range.

   Click as shown

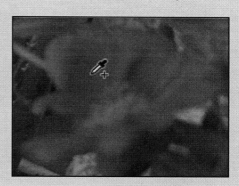

To add more of the flower color.

6  Observe the preview                         Some of the other red areas are probably
                                               included, but you want to make sure to include
                                               them all.

7  Increase Fuzziness to **200**

   Click **OK**                                To apply the selections.

8  Update the image                            Next, you'll adjust the hue and saturation.

## Color adjustments

*Explanation*

When you choose a command—such as Hue/Saturation—from the Image, Adjustments submenu, it opens a corresponding dialog box, where you can change settings. When you change an image in this way, the edits you make are *destructive;* that is, they change the image pixels.

To make the same kinds of adjustments—Hue/Saturation, Levels, Brightness/Contrast, and so on—but without changing the image pixels, you can use the Adjustments panel to add an *adjustment layer*. You can then easily remove that layer to return the image to its original appearance. In addition, you can continually modify an adjustment layer's settings to experiment with different values. Adjustment layers appear in the Layers panel, as shown in Exhibit 2-10.

You can blend adjustment types by applying different adjustments to the same layer or by applying different adjustments to different layers. Actually, because adjustment layers behave like other layers in Photoshop, you can group them, adjust their opacity, create clipping masks, and apply blending modes just as you would with other layers.

*Exhibit 2-10: Adjustment layers*

### Global hue changes

There are several ways to change a specific color throughout an image:

- Create a Selective Color adjustment layer. Selective Color is intended primarily for CMYK printed images. You can adjust the amount of cyan, magenta, yellow, and black used to create red, green, blue, cyan, magenta, yellow, white, neutrals, and grays. For example, you can specify that greens should contain more yellow to change the appearance of a lawn in an image without affecting the house.

- Create a duplicate layer. Then choose Image, Adjustments, Replace Color to open the Replace Color dialog box. Use the eyedropper tools and the Fuzziness slider in the dialog box to select a range of colors, and then drag Hue, Saturation, and Lightness sliders to shift the selection.

- A slightly more flexible variation on the previous approach is to choose Select, Color Range and select the colors as you would in the Replace Color dialog box. Then, with this selection active, create a Hue/Saturation adjustment layer.

- Use a Hue/Saturation adjustment layer by itself to restrict the affected color range, and change the hue, saturation, and lightness. This approach often creates the most realistic results because you can precisely control the range of the hue to be changed, as well as how large a range of transition colors to blend. Other approaches often create excessively sharp transitions between changed and unchanged colors.

To change one hue throughout an image with a Hue/Saturation adjustment layer:

1  In the Adjustments panel, click the Hue/Saturation icon to create an adjustment layer and display the Hue/Saturation options in the Properties panel, as shown in Exhibit 2-11.

2  From the Edit list, select the color closest to the one you want to change (it doesn't have to match exactly).

3  If you want to more accurately select the color to be changed, do a combination of the following:

   - Drag the color fall-off sliders between the color ramps to expand or narrow the number of transition colors to be affected. The colors between the vertical bars and the color fall-off sliders are partially affected by the adjustments.

   - Drag the vertical sliders between the color ramps to the left and right of the gray area to expand or narrow the range of colors to be shifted.

   - Drag the gray area between the color ramps to shift the hue.

   - Select the Eyedropper tool and click in the image to select the color you want to change. If you click a color very different from the one you selected from the Edit list, the color in the Edit list will change.

   - Add to or subtract from the range of colors with the + and – Eyedropper tools. (Or press Shift to temporarily access the + Eyedropper, and press Alt to temporarily access the – Eyedropper.)

4  Drag the Hue, Saturation, and Lightness sliders to affect the selected color range.

5  If necessary, select the Hue/Saturation layer's layer mask thumbnail, and paint with black in an image area to prevent color changes from occurring there.

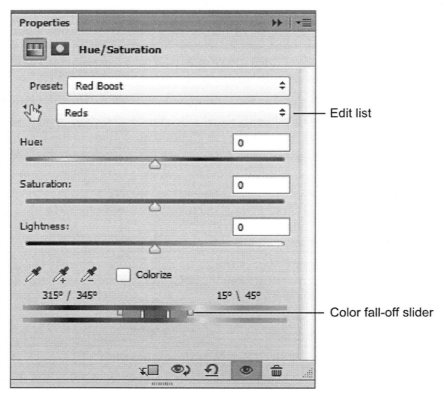

*Exhibit 2-11: The Hue/Saturation options in the Adjustments panel*

**Adjusting vibrance**

The Saturation adjustment is useful for increasing the impact of subtle colors, but it can make already saturated colors "clip," or exceed their maximum values. The *Vibrance* adjustment takes this into consideration by applying less adjustment to the more saturated portions of the image. This feature is especially useful for images that contain skin tones that you do not want to over-saturate.

*Do it!*        **C-3:   Changing color by using adjustment layers**

| Here's how | Here's why |
|---|---|
| 1  In the Adjustments panel, click 🖼 | (The Hue/Saturation button.) To add a Hue/Saturation adjustment layer to the image and to open the Properties panel. The selected areas are converted to a mask, so the adjustments you make will apply only to those areas. |
| 2  Drag the Hue slider all the way to the left | Observe the image colors changing as you drag. |
|     Set the Hue value to **-20** | To make the reds more purple. |
| 3  Drag the Saturation slider to the right | To increase the saturation in the image, making the hue more intense. |
|     Set the Saturation value to **+20** | |
| 4  At the bottom of the panel, click 👁 | To toggle the layer's visibility. |
|     Click the button several times | To see the difference between the original and adjusted images. You'll try a preset. |
|     Make the Hue/Saturation layer visible | |
| 5  In the Properties panel, from the Preset list, select **Red Boost** | |
| 6  In the Adjustments panel, click ▽ | To add a Vibrance adjustment layer and to display the Vibrance settings in the Properties panel. |
| 7  Drag the Saturation slider all the way to the right | The more saturated colors become garish. |
|     In the Properties panel, click ↺ | To reset the adjustment defaults. |
| 8  Drag the Vibrance slider all the way to the left | To observe the effect of this adjustment. |
| 9  Update the image | |

## Colorizing

*Explanation*

You can use the Hue/Saturation dialog box to adjust a color image's hue, saturation, and lightness. You can apply a Hue/Saturation adjustment to an entire layer or to selected pixels within a layer. In addition, you can specify that the adjustment should affect only pixels within a particular color range.

You can also use the Hue/Saturation dialog box to *colorize* an image, adding a single color hue to an image so that it appears as if that color had been added to a grayscale image. This technique is useful when you want to add a single color to a black and white or desaturated image for emphasis.

To colorize an image:

1   Create a Hue/Saturation layer or select an existing one.
2   In the Properties panel, check Colorize.
3   Specify Hue, Saturation, and Lightness values.

*Do it!*          **C-4:   Colorizing an image**

| Here's how | Here's why |
|---|---|
| 1  In the Layers panel, select the **Hue/Saturation 1** layer |  |
|  | Unhappy with the hue/saturation and vibrance adjustments, you decide to try colorizing the image. |
| 2  In the Properties panel, check **Colorize** | To convert the pixels to a different hue while retaining the image's general appearance. |
| 3  Set the Saturation value to **50** | So that you can more easily see the effects of the Hue adjustment. |
| 4  Drag the Hue slider all the way to the left | (So the value is zero.) To add a red hue. |
|    Slowly drag the Hue slider all the way to the right | To progress through the gradations of hues. The color shifts from red to orange, yellow, green, blue, indigo, violet, and finally back to red. |
| 5  Adjust the Hue value so that the selection has a green tint | A value of about 100 achieves the desired effect. |
| 6  Drag the Saturation slider all the way to the left | To reduce the saturation of the image completely, creating a black-and-white image. |
|    Slowly drag the Saturation slider all the way to the right | To increase the saturation of the specified hue. |
|    Set the Saturation value to **30** | To set the Saturation value so that the hue is noticeable but not overwhelming. |
|  | You want this adjustment to apply to the whole image. |
| 7  In the Layers panel, click the Hue/Saturation 1 layer mask thumbnail, as shown |  |
|    Press (ALT) and click | To delete the layer mask, but not the layer itself. The whole image is now colorized. |
| 8  Minimize the Properties panel |  |
| 9  Update the image |  |

## Spot colors

*Explanation*

Printing full-color images by combining cyan, magenta, yellow, and black inks is typically called *four-color printing* or *process printing*. When you're printing a document that uses three or fewer solid colors, you can instead print those images by using spot colors.

A *spot color* is a premixed ink color that is printed on its own printing plate. The more printing plates that are needed to print a publication, the higher the printing costs are. Therefore, spot colors are typically used in addition to black in publications with fewer than four inks. You can also use spot colors for colors you can't generate by combining cyan, magenta, yellow, and black, such as vibrant blues and greens or metallic colors, or for very specific colors, such as those in a company logo.

Spot colors in Photoshop are stored in channels, which you view in the Channels panel. If you create a new channel from an active selection, the channel is created from the selection. If no selection is active, then Photoshop creates an empty channel.

To specify a spot color in Photoshop:

1. From the Channels panel menu, choose New Spot Channel to open the New Spot Channel dialog box, shown in Exhibit 2-12.

2. Click the color swatch to open the Color Picker (Spot Color) dialog box. To select a color from a color library, such as Pantone, click Color Libraries. From the Book list in the Color Libraries dialog box, select the color matching system you want to use. Then select a swatch and click OK.

3. In the Solidity box, enter a percentage based on the level of transparency you expect the ink to show when printed. The Solidity value affects only onscreen display, not printing.

4. Click OK.

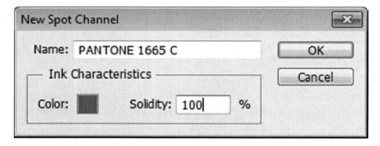

*Exhibit 2-12: The New Spot Channel dialog box*

### Ink overprinting and solidity

Pantone inks tend to be opaque, hiding what's printed beneath them. Like the other process inks (cyan, magenta, and yellow), black is semi-transparent, so other inks can show through. That's why adding 100% magenta and 100% yellow makes red, for example, not just 100% of whichever ink was printed on top.

The New Spot Channel dialog box's Solidity setting helps you visualize the effect of blending inks together. It affects only the onscreen display in Photoshop, not the printed output. You should refer to a printed sample, such as a Pantone color guide with combinations of inks at different percentages, because guessing the Solidity value might produce unwanted results.

To avoid potential problems—such as black being printed after a spot color, making an overlapping area look dark and muddy—you might want to "knock out" the black from the area where the spot color resides. You can do this by creating a layer mask or filling with white, as shown in Exhibit 2-13.

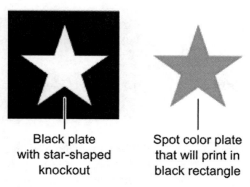

Black plate
with star-shaped
knockout

Spot color plate
that will print in
black rectangle

*Exhibit 2-13: A white area knocked out of the black plate so no black ink will overlap the spot color ink*

### Saving images with spot colors

When you create an image that includes spot colors, you must save it in a format that retains those colors before you can use the image in a page layout application.

The DCS (Desktop Color Separation), TIFF, PSD, PDF, PSB and RAW formats support both process colors and spot colors. The DCS 1.0 format creates a separate file for each color channel, but this is rarely necessary. The DCS 2.0 format, a variant of the EPS (Encapsulated PostScript) format, is more commonly used and is more compatible with other applications for spot-color printing than are the other formats.

*Do it!*

## C-5:   Adding a spot-color channel

| Here's how | Here's why |
|---|---|
| 1  Select the **Horizontal Type Mask Tool**, as indicated | T. ■ T Horizontal Type Tool    T<br>↓T Vertical Type Tool    T<br>T Horizontal Type Mask Tool    T<br>↓T Vertical Type Mask Tool    T |
|  | Since spot channels don't interact directly with layers, you'll create a type mask. |
| Set the type format to **Arial, Bold Italic, 80 pt** |  |
| 2  Click in the image and type **Get ahead...plant today!** |  |
| Click ✓ | (On the options bar.) To convert the type into a selection. |
| Press (M) to select a Marquee tool, and drag the selection from within its edges to the bottom of the image |  |

| | |
|---|---|
| 3  Click the **Channels** panel tab | |
| From the Channels panel menu, choose **New Spot Channel...** | To open the New Spot Channel dialog box. |
| 4  Click the color swatch | To open the Color Picker (Spot Color) dialog box. You'll select a color from a Pantone library. |
| Click **Color Libraries** | To open the Color Libraries dialog box. |
| Type **1665** | To select PANTONE 1665 C as the color. |
| Click **OK** | To return to the New Spot Channel dialog box. |
| 5  Set the Solidity value to **100%** | The Solidity value affects only the onscreen display, not printing. It reflects the level of transparency you expect the ink to show when printed. |
| | Pantone ink is typically opaque, so it would replace the color in the picture if it were printed after the black ink, as it appears at the 100% setting. If the Pantone ink were printed first, however, the black ink from the image would darken the letters, as it appears in Photoshop with low Solidity values. |
| | To prevent the color from looking like 0% solidity (with black darkening the words) when printed, you'll knock out the gray ink where it overlaps the spot color. Then it won't matter which ink prints first. |
| Click **OK** | To close the New Spot Channel dialog box. Since there was a selection active in the image, the spot color was applied to it. |
| 6  Press (CTRL) and click the PANTONE 1665 C channel's thumbnail | To convert the PANTONE 1665 C channel to a selection. |
| Choose **Select**, **Modify**, **Contract...** | To open the Contract Selection dialog box. |
| Edit the Contract By box to read **1** | (If necessary.) To allow for a slight overlap of inks for trapping. |
| Click **OK** | |

7  In the Layers panel, create a new
   layer

   Press (D)                                   To set the foreground and background colors to
                                               their defaults.

   Press (CTRL) + (← BACKSPACE)                To fill the selection in the new layer with the
                                               white background color.

8  In the Channels panel, hide the            To view the knockout you created in the
   PANTONE 1665 C channel                      grayscale version.

   Show the PANTONE 1665 C                     To turn it back on.
   channel

   Press (CTRL) + (D)                          To deselect.

9  Zoom in on the word Get at 500%            To examine the edges.
   magnification

   Deselect the selection

10 Double-click to the right of the           To open the Spot Channel Options dialog box.
   name for the PANTONE 1665 C
   channel

   Set the Solidity value to **0**

                                               To see the 1-pixel overlap between the Pantone
                                               ink and the grayscale image. This overlap will
                                               prevent a white gap from appearing if the
                                               Pantone ink is shifted relative to the black ink
                                               when the image is printed.

   Click **Cancel**                           To keep the Solidity value set to 100%.

11 With the Move tool selected,               The Pantone ink shifts slightly compared to the
   press (→) twice                            background. No large white gap appears at the
                                               first nudge, but because the overlap you created
                                               is only 1 pixel, the white gap is clearly visible at
                                               the second nudge.

   Press (←) twice                            To move the Pantone ink back to its original
                                               position.

12 Update and close the image

### The Color Replacement tool

*Explanation*

You might want to replace a color in only certain places in an image, and that color might be interspersed with other colors, making it difficult to create an accurate mask or to paint in the new color with precision. The Color Replacement tool can easily replace colors in such images. It works much like the Magic Eraser tool, in that it changes only the pixels that match a target color as you paint.

To replace colors with the Color Replacement tool:

1 Create a duplicate layer so that the effects of this destructive edit can be reversed if necessary.

2 Set the foreground color to the color you want to use as the replacement.

3 Select the Color Replacement tool, which is located in the same tool group as the Brush tool.

4 On the options bar, use the Brush Preset picker to specify a brush size, or press [ and ] to change the size.

5 From the Mode list, select the blending mode (Hue, Saturation, Color, or Luminosity) with which the new color will replace the old one. In most cases, Color is most effective.

6 Click an icon to specify the sampling type you want to use:

- **Sampling: Continuous** — Changes the color of all pixels you drag across that match the color at the center of the pointer as you drag. This option works well for replacing varying colors as you paint.

- **Sampling: Once** — Changes only colors that match the color that was under the pointer when you began dragging. This option works well when the areas you want to replace are fairly consistent in color. You can stop dragging, and begin in a new location to begin replacing a different color.

- **Sampling: Background Swatch** — Replaces only colors that match the current background color, shown in the Background color indicator in the Tools panel. This option works well for images with a single color to replace.

7 From the Limits list, select a limits mode:

- **Discontiguous** — Replaces all instances of the sampled color located below the pointer as you drag.

- **Contiguous** — Replaces only instances of the sampled color that are connected to one another.

- **Find Edges** — Replaces connected areas of the sampled color while better preserving the sharpness of shape edges.

8 In the Tolerance box, specify a value to determine how similar to the sampled color other areas must be to be replaced. A low tolerance replaces only areas very similar to the sampled color, and a high tolerance replaces a broader range of colors.

9 Check Anti-alias if you want to soften brush-stroke edges; clear it if you don't want overlapping strokes to display a visible edge.

10 Drag over the areas containing the color that you want to replace

*Do it!*

## C-6: Replacing a color by painting

The files for this activity are in Student Data folder **Unit 2\Topic C**.

| Here's how | Here's why |
|---|---|
| 1 Open Red peppers | |
| Save the image as **My red and green peppers** | (In the current topic folder.) You'll change the pepper in the foreground from red to green. |
| 2 Duplicate the Background layer | To preserve it from a destructive edit. |
| 3 Click the foreground color | (In the Tools panel.) To open the Color Picker (Foreground Color) dialog box. |
| Move the slider to the indicated area | ⊙ H: 114 °  ○ S: 0 %  ○ B: 0 %  ○ R: 0  ○ G: 0  ○ B: 0 |
| Select a green color | |
| Click **OK** | |
| 4 Right-click the Brush tool and select the **Color Replacement Tool** | You'll paint in the new color rather than replace it throughout the entire image. |
| 5 Press ❑ as necessary to increase the brush size to 70 pixels | Press the Right Bracket key. |
| On the options bar, click 🖋 | (The Sampling: Once icon.) To replace colors based only on the color that's under the pointer when you *begin* dragging, not the colors under the pointer as you continue to drag. |
| Type **6** | To set the Tolerance to 60%. Increasing the tolerance will replace more shades of red. You don't need to worry about accidentally replacing similar colors, so you can safely increase the tolerance for this image. |
| On the options bar, clear **Anti-alias** | To avoid creating visible edges where your paint strokes overlap one another. |

6 Point as shown, with the crosshair within a red color and with the edge of the brush circle past the edge of the pepper

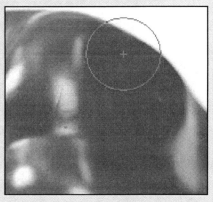

To choose the color (under the crosshair) to sample, and the area (within the circle) to paint.

Drag around the edge of the pepper as shown

To paint the outer edge of the pepper but not the colors surrounding it. Don't paint the background pepper.

7 Point as shown, and begin painting the inside of the pepper

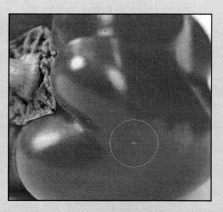

To sample a slightly lighter red so you can replace the light red color near the edges that meet the background pepper.

Paint the as much of the foreground pepper as you can, being careful not to extend the brush edge into the background pepper

Don't worry about replacing the stem color—the tool won't replace the stem color because it doesn't match the red you sampled.

| | |
|---|---|
| 8 Press [ eight times to reduce the brush size to 20 pixels | (Left Bracket.) You'll touch up the remaining areas with a smaller brush to avoid painting on the background pepper. |
| 9 Drag over the areas of the pepper that remain red, again being careful to keep the brush edge within the front pepper | To complete the color replacement. |
| 10 Update and close the image | |

# Unit summary: Working with color

*Topic A*    In this topic, you added colors to the **Swatches panel**, and you used fill shortcuts to fill selections and layers with color. In addition, you used **fill layers** to create layers filled with solid color.

*Topic B*    In this topic, you learned how to use the Gradient tool to add a **gradient** to a layer or selection. You also learned how to create a **gradient fill layer** to add a gradient to an image. Then you learned how to use **overlay layer styles** to fill layer content with a color, gradient, or pattern.

*Topic C*    In this topic, you selected color by using the **Magic Wand** tool and the **Color Range** command. You also used the Adjustments panel to change an image's **hue** and **saturation** and adjust **vibrance**. Then you used the Hue/Saturation dialog box to **colorize** an image, and you created a **spot-color channel**. Finally, you **replaced colors** throughout an image by using the Color Replacement tool.

## Review questions

1  True or false? In the Swatches panel, a swatch can consist of a color, pattern, or gradient.

2  To fill an image with color that automatically expands if you enlarge the canvas size, what should you create?

3  You want to add a gradient on the current layer. Which technique should you use?

   A  Choose Layer, New Fill Layer, Gradient.

   B  In the Layers panel, click the "Create new fill or adjustment layer" icon and choose Gradient.

   C  Select the Gradient tool, select a gradient from the Gradient Picker, and drag in the image.

   D  Select a gradient swatch in the Swatches panel and then press Alt+Delete to fill the layer with that gradient.

4  To create a gradient that automatically aligns with a type layer's contents even when you edit the text, what should you use?

5  What dialog box do overlays appear in?

6  Which of the following can you do with the Hue/Saturation dialog box? [Choose all that apply.]

   A  Change the brightness of the image's shadows, midtones, and highlights independently.

   B  Colorize an image.

   C  Make the image's colors more vibrant.

   D  Make an image's orange colors redder.

7   True or false? You can apply a Hue/Saturation adjustment to selected pixels on a layer or to an entire layer at once.

8   Which tool allows you to paint over multiple colors in an image, changing only the pixels that match a sample color?

A   The Magic Eraser tool.

B   The Color Replacement tool.

C   The Color Sampler tool.

D   The Brush tool.

9   Using the Color Replacement tool, you want to replace a range of colors as you paint in the image. Which option should you select?

A   Color Sampling: Continuous

B   Color Sampling: Once

C   Color Sampling: Background Swatch

D   Anti-alias

## Independent practice activity

In this activity, you'll create custom swatches and use them to apply a gradient overlay. You'll also select color and adjust it, and you'll colorize a layer. Finally, you'll add a spot-color channel to the image.

The files for this activity are in Student Data folder **Unit 2\Unit summary**.

1   Open Peppers background and save the image as **My peppers background**.

2   Create three swatches by sampling the yellow color from the carrot in the logo—the original color, one lighter, and one darker. Name the new colors **Harvest Valley yellow**, **Lighter HV yellow**, and **Darker HV yellow**.

3   On the Background layer, add a gradient overlay that blends from the Darker HV yellow color to the Lighter HV yellow color.

4   Select the blue background in the logo. (*Hint*: Use a color-selection tool or command. Be sure to select the blue within the letters.)

5   Add a Hue/Saturation adjustment layer above the Market logo layer. Apply the **Old Style** preset to the adjustment layer.

6   Colorize the Peppers layer, but not the Background layer. Give the peppers a yellowish color to match the background. (*Hint*: Create a clipping mask.)

7   Select the black color in the text PEPPERS. (*Hint*: Don't use a type tool to select the type.)

8   Add a spot-color channel that uses the color **PANTONE 7403 C**.

9   Hide the PEPPERS text layer.

10  Update and close the image.

# Unit 3

## Masks

Complete this unit, and you'll know how to:

**A** Paint in Quick Mask mode and in an alpha channel to specify a selection.

**B** Create a layer mask to hide part of a layer, and use grayscale masks to partially mask part of an image.

**C** Refine a selection by using the Refine Edge dialog box.

# Topic A: Mask channels

This topic covers the following ACE exam objectives for Photoshop CS6.

| # | Objective |
|---|---|
| **4.3** | **Quick Mask usage** |
| 4.3.1 | Creating a Quick Mask from a selection |
| 4.3.2 | Creating a blank Quick Mask |
| 4.3.3 | Changing overlay |
| 4.3.4 | Using brushes for addition to Quick Mask |
| 4.3.5 | Saving selections |

## Using masks

*Explanation*

When you select part of an image, the areas outside the selection are *masked*, because you can't paint in those areas. This concept is similar to a painter using masking tape to cover areas that should not be painted.

In addition to using Photoshop's selection tools to select image areas, you can use painting tools to select areas. The painting tools can be more intuitive than the selection tools and can make it easier to add to or subtract from a complex selection. To specify image selections by painting, you can paint in Quick Mask mode or in an alpha channel.

## Quick Masks

One way to create a selection by painting is to use *Quick Mask mode*. This mode displays a semi-transparent colored overlay to differentiate between selected and non-selected areas.

To activate Quick Mask mode, click the Edit in Quick Mask Mode button in the Tools panel or press Q. To return to Standard mode (in which a selection appears as a marquee), click the Edit in Standard Mode button or press Q.

If you already have a selection active in the image, Photoshop bases the Quick Mask on the selection. By default, the color overlay appears over all areas of the image that are not selected (the masked areas), although you can reverse this.

You can also create a blank Quick Mask. If you click the Edit in Quick Mask Mode button without first making a selection, Photoshop creates a new blank channel in the Channels panel.

In Quick Mask mode, you can use the painting tools to add to or subtract from the selection (or to create a mask, if no selection is active). In its default configuration, painting with black adds to the masked area, and painting with white adds to the selected area.

By default, the masking overlay is red. If that's difficult to distinguish from the image itself, you can change the masking color. To change the overlay:

1 Double-click the Edit in Quick Mask Mode button to open the Quick Mask Options dialog box, shown in Exhibit 3-1.

2 Click the color swatch to open the Select Quick Mask Color dialog box.

3 Specify the color you want to use, and click OK.

4 Under Color, adjust the Opacity value, if necessary.

5 Click OK.

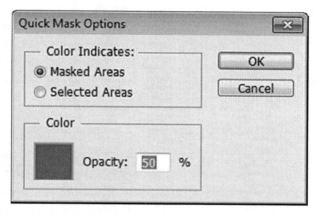

*Exhibit 3-1: The Quick Mask Options dialog box*

*Do it!*

### A-1:   Editing a Quick Mask

The files for this activity are in Student Data folder **Unit 3\Topic A**.

| Here's how | Here's why |
|---|---|
| 1  Open Rhinos 1 | |
| Save the image as **My rhinos 1** | You'll select the rhinos, and then you'll clean up the selection by painting in Quick Mask mode. |
| 2  Select the Lasso tool | |
| 3  Very quickly, draw a selection marquee around the rhinos, as shown | Don't worry about creating an extremely accurate selection; you'll clean up the selection in Quick Mask mode. |

4  At the bottom of the Tools panel, click 🔲

(The Edit in Quick Mask Mode button.) To enter Quick Mask mode. The unselected areas of the image appear as transparent red. You'll now paint in Quick Mask mode to fine-tune the selection.

5  Press (D)

(If necessary.) To set the foreground and background colors to their defaults.

6  Select the Brush tool

Display the Brush Preset picker

On the options bar.

Specify a Size setting of **20 px**

Specify a Hardness setting of **100%**

Press (↵ ENTER)

To close the Brush Preset picker.

7  Paint any areas that should be masked

(That is, paint those areas around the hippos that should *not* be part of the selection.) Painting with black adds to the masked area.

8  Press (X)

To switch the foreground and background colors. Painting with white subtracts from the masked area.

Paint the areas of the hippos that should be visible but are masked with red

9  As necessary, press (X) to switch the foreground and background colors as you touch up the mask

Zoom in and adjust the brush size as necessary.

10  Update the image

## Saving and loading selections

*Explanation*

After you select part of an image, you might want to choose the same area again later. To be able to do this, you can save the selection. After saving a selection, you can deselect it and then load it again at any time.

A saved selection is stored in the Channels panel, shown in Exhibit 3-2. The Channels panel stores color information about an image, as well as selections. Additional channels you add to the Channels panel are known as *alpha channels*. The white part of an alpha channel represents the part of the image that will be selected when you load the channel.

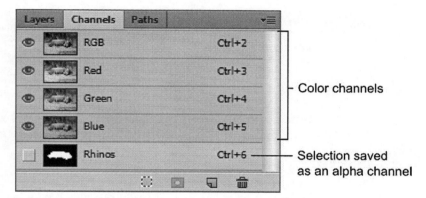

*Exhibit 3-2: A selection stored in the Channels panel*

There are two ways you can save the current selection:

- Choose Select, Save Selection to open the Save Selection dialog box. Enter a name for the selection and click OK.
- At the bottom of the Channels panel, click the "Save selection as channel" button.

After you deselect a selection, you can load it again. Here are two ways to do so:

- Choose Select, Load Selection to open the Load Selection dialog box. From the Channel list, select the saved selection you want to load. Then click OK.
- In the Channels panel, press Ctrl and click the thumbnail next to the alpha channel you want to load as a selection.

*Do it!*

## A-2: Saving and loading a selection

| Here's how | Here's why |
|---|---|
| 1 At the bottom of the Tools panel, click ▢ | To return to Standard Mode. The selection reflects the Quick Mask you edited. |
| 2 Choose **Select**, **Save Selection...** | To open the Save Selection dialog box. |
| In the Name box, enter **Rhinos** | |
| Click **OK** | To save the selection as an alpha channel. After you have saved a selection, you can load it at any time. |
| Deselect the current selection | |
| 3 Choose **Select**, **Load Selection...** | To open the Load Selection dialog box. "Rhinos" is already selected in the Channel list. |
| Click **OK** | To load the selection. |
| Deselect the current selection | Another way to load a selection is to select it from the Channels panel. Each selection is saved as a separate channel. |
| 4 In the Layers panel group, click the **Channels** panel | (If necessary.) The selected area is represented by the white portion of the Rhinos channel. |
| Press and hold ⌈CTRL⌋, and click the Rhinos channel | ▢ 🚗 Rhinos ⬚ Ctrl+6 |
| | To load the selection. When you press Ctrl and point to the channel, the mouse pointer changes to indicate that you'll load the selection. |
| Deselect the current selection | |
| 5 Click the **Rhinos** channel | To display the alpha channel in the image window. |
| Click the **RGB** channel | To display the image. |
| 6 Update and close the image | |

# Topic B:  Layer masks

This topic covers the following ACE exam objectives for Photoshop CS6.

| # | Objective |
|---|---|
| **5.3** | **Understanding layer masks** |
| 5.3.1 | Creating layer masks using Panels and shortcuts |
| 5.3.2 | Modifying layer masks using brush-based tools |
| 5.3.3 | Copying and moving layer masks |
| 5.3.4 | Understanding the relationship between layer masks and Quick Mask |
| 5.3.5 | Using layer masks with vector images and type |
| **6.3** | **Refining masks on adjustments** |
| 6.3.1 | Refining masks using the Density, Mask Edge, and Refine Mask options found in the Mask Properties panel |

## Creating layer masks

*Explanation*

When you want to show only part of a layer's contents, you can create a *layer mask*. That way, you can change which part of the layer is visible in the image at any time, or you can reveal the entire layer again if necessary.

To create a layer mask, first select the part of the layer that you want to show. The unselected area will be hidden by the layer mask. Then, at the bottom of the Layers panel, click the Add layer mask button. The Layers panel will display a layer thumbnail and a layer mask thumbnail for that layer, as shown in Exhibit 1-2.

In contrast to a Quick Mask, a layer mask hides and shows areas in the image so that you can work with the transparent areas, for example, to show parts of other layers, while retaining the masked area. To remove a layer mask, click the layer mask thumbnail and press Delete.

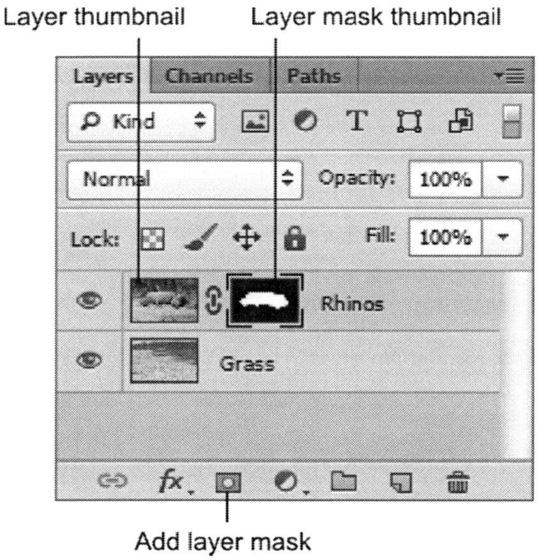

Layer thumbnail    Layer mask thumbnail

Add layer mask

*Exhibit 3-3: A layer containing a layer mask*

*Do it!*

## B-1: Creating a layer mask

The files for this activity are in Student Data folder **Unit 3\Topic B**.

| Here's how | Here's why |
|---|---|
| 1 Open Rhinos 2 | |
| Save the image as **My rhinos 2** | In the current topic folder. You'll use a layer mask to isolate the rhinos from the background. |
| 2 Click the **Channels** panel | If necessary. |
| Press (CTRL) and click the **Rhinos** channel | To load the channel as a selection. |
| 3 Click the **Layers** panel | |
| Select the **Rhinos** layer | |
| Click  [□] | (The Add layer mask button.) To add a layer mask for the unselected area of the image. The Grass layer shows through the masked areas of the Rhinos layer. |
| 4 Observe the Rhinos layer in the Layers panel |  The layer now has both a layer thumbnail and a layer mask thumbnail. |
| 5 Update the image | |

### Editing layer masks

*Explanation*

After applying a layer mask to hide part of a layer, you might want to modify the layer mask. To add to or subtract from a layer mask, activate it by clicking the layer mask thumbnail. Otherwise, you'll be painting over the layer pixels themselves. When you activate the layer mask, the image's appearance in the image window doesn't change. However, when you paint with black in the image, you add to the mask (subtracting from the selection), and when you paint with white, you add to the selection.

To return to editing the image itself, click the image thumbnail in the Layers panel. In addition, use the following techniques to change your view of the layer mask thumbnail:

- To view the layer mask in the image window, press Alt and click the layer mask thumbnail.
- To view the image in the image window, click the layer thumbnail or press Alt and click the layer mask thumbnail.
- To disable the layer mask, revealing the entire layer, press Shift and click the layer mask thumbnail.
- To enable the layer mask, hiding the masked areas, press Shift and click the layer mask thumbnail again.

#### Copying and moving layer masks

You can copy or move existing layer masks to new layers. To copy a layer mask, press Ctrl and click the mask to convert it to a selection. Then select the layer where you want to copy the mask and click the Add layer mask button. To move a layer mask from one layer to another, simply drag the layer mask thumbnail to the desired layer.

#### Mask properties

You can change many layer mask options by using the Properties panel, shown in Exhibit 3-4. In the Properties panel, you can click Mask Edge to open the Refine Mask dialog box. This dialog box contains the same options as the Refine Edge dialog box.

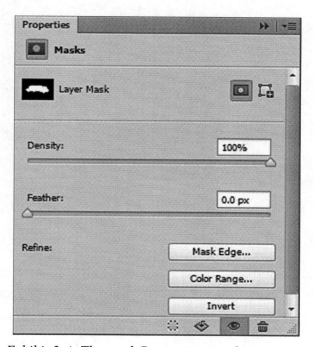

*Exhibit 3-4: The mask Properties panel*

*Do it!*

## B-2: Editing a layer mask

| Here's how | Here's why |
|---|---|
| 1 Double-click the layer mask thumbnail | To open the Properties panel. |
| | You want to remove some areas of the mask so that the rocks in the original image show through, but you can't see them to know where to paint. |
| Set the Density to **40%** | So that you can see the rocks in the Rhinos layer and also some detail in the Grass layer. |
| Minimize the Properties panel | |
| 2 Select the Brush tool | |
| Set the brush size to **100** | |
| Press ⒟ | To set the foreground and background colors to their defaults. |
| Observe the default foreground and background colors | |
| | (In the Tools panel.) When a layer mask is selected, the default foreground color is white, and the default background color is black. |
| Paint with white over the rocks, as shown | To remove the area from the mask. |

| | |
|---|---|
| 3 Double-click the layer mask thumbnail | |
| Set the Density to **100%** | To completely hide the masked areas. |
| | You want to refine the mask to make the edges less sharp. |

| | |
|---|---|
| 4 Click **Mask Edge** | To open the Refine Mask dialog box. |
| From the View list, select **On Layers** | To see the layer below the mask as you edit. |
| Press (ESC) | |
| 5 Set the Radius to **2.0** | To increase the size of the refiniement area. |
| Set the Smooth value to **20** | To smooth the jagged edges. |
| Press (P) | To show the original mask. |
| Press (P) again | To show the refined mask. |
| 6 Click **OK** | To close the dialog box. |
| Minimize the Properties panel | |
| 7 Press (ALT) and click the layer mask thumbnail | To view the mask. There might be some areas that you missed. |
| Paint with white or black | To remove or add and "stray" areas to the mask. |
| Click the layer thumbnail | To return to viewing the image. You'll copy the mask to the Grass layer. |
| 8 Press (CTRL) and click the layer mask thumbnail | To load it as a selection. |
| Select the **Grass** layer | |
| Click [▣] | To convert the selection to a layer mask. |
| Hide the Rhinos layer | To see the mask on the Grass layer. |
| 9 Press (SHIFT) and click the Grass layer mask thumbnail | |

To disable the layer mask. A red "X" appears over the layer mask thumbnail, and the entire layer is visible.

| | |
|---|---|
| 10 Show the Rhinos layer | |
| Right-click the Rhinos layer mask thumbnail | |
| Choose **Delete Layer Mask** | |
| 11 Drag the layer mask from the Grass layer to the Rhinos layer | To move it. Photoshop enables it automatically. |
| 12 Update the image | |

## The Type Mask tool

Yet another way to create a mask is to use the Horizontal and Vertical Type Mask tools, located in the group with the Horizontal Type tool. Essentially, these tools create a selection in the shape of the text you type, rather than a separate type layer. Once you're finished editing the text, you can apply adjustments either to the selection or to the image outside of the selection. You can save the selection as a channel so that you can use it later.

## Masking with vector paths

When you want to select or mask part of an image that has a geometric shape or is very detailed, you'll often get more accurate results by using vector paths. You can't directly use a vector path to partially mask image pixels, as you can by painting with gray in an alpha channel, in a pixel-based layer mask, or in Quick Mask mode. However, after creating a path in the shape of the area you want to select or mask, you can convert the vector path to a selection or layer mask.

*Do it!*                    **B-3:   Creating a type mask**

| Here's how | Here's why |
|---|---|
| 1  Select the Rhinos layer mask thumbnail | |
| 2  Right-click the Horizontal Type tool and select the **Horizontal Type Mask Tool** | |
| 3  Click the left side of the image | To create a mask. |
| Specify a font of **Arial**, **Black**, **200 pt** | |
| On the options bar, click [≡] | To left-align the text. |
| Type **RHINOS** | |
| 4  Point away from the selection | |
| | The pointer indicates that you can move the mask. |
| Drag the text to the bottom of the image | To center it in the grassy area. |
| 5  On the options bar, click [✓] | To commit the edits. The type becomes a selection. |
| 6  In the Channels panel, press (ALT) and click [▣] | |
| Name the channel **RHINOS text** and click **OK** | To save the selection as a channel so that you can reuse it later, if desired. |
| 7  Press (D) | |
| 8  Press (ALT) + (← BACKSPACE) | To fill the selection with the foreground color (white), removing it from the mask. |
| Deselect the selection | |
| 9  Update the image | |

## Grayscale masks

*Explanation*

You can paint with white and black in a mask to add to and subtract from a selection. However, you might want to create a layer mask that has soft or feathered edges. To specify a soft or feathered edge in a mask, apply a gray color. In a mask, shades of gray represent regions that are partially masked. Partially masked areas appear semi-transparent. The darker the gray color, the more transparent the layer contents will be through the mask.

To specify soft or feathered edges in a mask, you can use several techniques:

- Convert a feathered selection to a mask.
- Paint in the layer mask with a soft-edged brush.
- Apply a blur filter to the layer mask.
- Use the Properties panel to feather the mask.

### Gradient masks

Another way to create a grayscale mask is to apply a gradient to part or all of a layer mask. Applying a gradient to a layer mask is useful when you want layer content to gradually fade across a specific area, rather than just display softened edges. For example, you might want to combine two images, with one fading gradually into the other. To apply a gradient to a layer mask:

1 Create a layer mask.
2 Select the Gradient tool.
3 In the Gradient picker (on the options bar), select the Black, White gradient.
4 In the Layers panel, verify that the layer mask thumbnail is selected.
5 Drag across the image to specify the area you want to fade.

*Do it!*     **B-4: Creating soft edges with a grayscale mask**

| Here's how | Here's why |
|---|---|
| 1  Click the layer mask thumbnail | |
| 2  Select the Brush tool | |
| 3  In the Brush Preset picker, set the Size to **50 px** and the Hardness to **0%** | |
| Set the Opacity to **75%** | On the options bar. |
| 4  Press ⟨D⟩ | |
| 5  Draw around the bottom edge of the rhinos and rocks, as shown | |

| | |
|---|---|
| 6  Select the Gradient tool | |
| From the Gradient picker, select the **Black, White** gradient |  |
| 7  Drag from the left edge of the image to the right edge | To see the effect of applying a gradient mask. The two layers blend together. |
| Press ⟨CTRL⟩ + ⟨Z⟩ | To undo the gradient mask. |
| 8  Update and close the image | |

# Topic C: Refine selections and masks

This topic covers the following ACE exam objectives for Photoshop CS6.

| # | Objective |
|---|---|
| **4.4** | **Using Refine Edge** |
| 4.4.1 | Adjusting feather and smart radius |
| 4.4.2 | Masking to new layers or new channels |
| 4.4.3 | Determining which images will best be served by Refine Edge |
| 4.4.4 | Creating selections that will best benefit from Refine Edge |

## The Refine Edge dialog box

*Explanation*

Although a selection might appear relatively smooth, it might contain jagged areas, or the edge of it might overlap areas that you want to leave out. You can modify a selection by adding to it, subtracting from it, expanding and contracting it, and feathering it until you have selected the desired area of the image. However, you might want even more control over the quality of a selection's edges. After you've made a selection, you can fine-tune it by using the Refine Edge dialog box, shown in Exhibit 3-5, to adjust the Radius, Contrast, Smooth, Feather, and Contract/Expand settings.

Images that have a sharp contrast between the selection and the surrounding area will work best when using Refine Edge. When making a selection, try to select as much of the area that you ultimately want to include—you might need to use a combination of selection tools to make sure all the detail you want in the selection is included.

To begin using the Refine Edge dialog box, first make or load a selection. Then either choose Select, Refine Edge or click Refine Edge on the options bar. By default, the image changes to show the selection over a white background, hiding the image areas that are not selected. The following table explains some of the settings in the Refine Edge dialog box.

| Setting | Description |
|---|---|
| Radius | Adjusts the area around the selection boundary in which edge refinement settings are applied. Check Smart Radius to automatically adjust the selection for hard and soft areas in the border to make selections around soft areas softer and make selections around hard areas harder. |
| Smooth | Reduces the jagged appearance of a selection edge. |
| Feather | Blends a selection edge with its background by applying transparency to the selection's surrounding pixels. |
| Contrast | Sharpens the selection edge. For example, if the Radius setting is high, the selection edge might appear fuzzy; you can increase the Contrast setting to reduce the "noise." |
| Shift Edge | Reduces or enlarges the selection boundary. |
| Decontaminate Colors | Reduces color fringes by replacing them with the color from nearby pixels. The softness of the selection edge affects the strength of the color replacement. |

The Refine Edge dialog box, shown in Exhibit 3-5, also contains two tools—the Refine Radius tool and the Erase Refinements tool. Use these tools to precisely adjust the selection border for a part of the image that otherwise would be difficult or impossible to select. For example, you could use the Refine Radius tool to select strands of hair over a background.

As you're making adjustments in the Refine Edge dialog box, it might help to view the image on different backgrounds. To do so, click View and select an option. For example, if the image within the selection is distracting, select Black & White to show the selection as a solid white area over a black background.

Refine Radius and
Erase Refinements tools

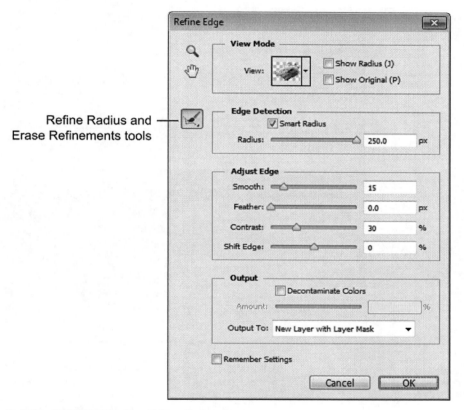

*Exhibit 3-5: The Refine Edge dialog box*

*Do it!*

## C-1: Using the Refine Edge dialog box

The files for this activity are in Student Data folder **Unit 3\Topic C**.

| Here's how | Here's why |
|---|---|
| 1 Open Chick | |
| Save the image as **My chick** | (In the current topic folder.) You want to create a layer mask to show a different background. You've made a selection, but you want to refine the selection to include more detail from the chick's feathers. |
| 2 Click the **Channels** panel | |
| Press (CTRL) and click the **Chick selection** channel | To load the selection. |
| Zoom to Actual Pixels and observe the selection | |

|  | It contains most of the chick's feathers but leaves out some of them. The selection also includes some of the background, which you want to eliminate. The edges you want to include in the selection are soft and fuzzy, rather than fine and sharp. |
|---|---|
| 3 Choose **Select, Refine Edge...** | To open the Refine Edge dialog box. The selected area appears in the image over a white background. |
| 4 Press (W) | (If necessary.) To change the View to On White. |
| Press (F) | To switch to the Black & White view mode. |
| Press (F) again | To switch to the On Layers view mode. The layer behind the selected layer shows outside of the current selection edge, as if the selection were a layer mask. |

5  Under Edge Detection, check **Smart Radius**

To automatically adjust the selection for soft and hard areas.

Drag the Radius slider to the right

To smooth the selection and include more of the feathers. You'll use a larger Radius setting because the selection edges are smooth and fuzzy.

Drag the Radius slider all the way to the right

To set the Radius to 250.0 px. This setting nearly achieves the desired result. However, there are still some areas that need to be refined.

6  In the Refine Edge dialog box, verify that the Refine Radius tool is selected

On the options bar, edit the Size box to read **20**

Point to the indicated area

(Above the chick's head.) You'll tell Photoshop to eliminate as much of this color as possible.

Click the fuzzy green area and then drag around the feathers

To use the Refine Radius tool to adjust the selection edge. When you release the mouse, Photoshop refines the selection edge to eliminate the unwanted area.

| | | |
|---|---|---|
| 7 | Continue using the Refine Radius tool to refine the selection | Drag around the chick's head until you've eliminated most of the original background. |
| 8 | Increase the Contrast setting | To eliminate some of the haze around the selection. |
| | Set the Contrast to about **30** | Some of the original detail is recovered. |
| 9 | Drag the Smooth slider to the right | To smooth the jagged edges of the selection. |
| | Set the Smooth value to about **15** | |
| 10 | Press `P` | To view the original selection. |
| | Press `P` again | To show the refined selection. |
| 11 | Press `J` | To see the area affected by your refinements. |
| | Press `J` again | |
| 12 | From the Output To list, select **New Layer with Layer Mask** | To create a new layer and layer mask from the refined selection. |
| 13 | Click **OK** | |
| 14 | Fit the image in the window | |
| | Click the **Layers** panel | To see the new layer and mask. |
| | Update and close the image | |

# Unit summary: Masks

**Topic A**　In this topic, you painted in **Quick Mask mode** to add to and subtract from a selection. You also learned how to **save and load** selections.

**Topic B**　In this topic, you created a **layer mask** to hide part of a layer. You also modified a layer mask. Then you used the **Horizontal Type Mask** tool to create a mask from text. You also created a **grayscale mask** to partially mask a portion of an image.

**Topic C**　In this topic, you used the **Refine Edge** dialog box to modify a selection, including detail you couldn't select with the selection tools.

## Review questions

1 How can you view a selection as a temporary colored overlay instead of as a marquee?

A In the Tools panel, click the Edit in Quick Mask Mode button.

B Choose View, Extras.

C Choose View, Show, Selection Edges to uncheck it.

D Choose View, Show, None.

2 In Quick Mask mode, how can you add to a selection?

A Choose Select, Modify, Expand.

B Choose Select, Grow.

C Paint with white.

D Paint with black.

3 How can you use the Channels panel to add to a saved selection?

A While viewing the image, Ctrl+click the alpha channel containing the selection; then paint with white.

B While viewing the image, Ctrl+click the alpha channel containing the selection; then paint with black.

C Click the alpha channel containing the selection to display it in the image window; then paint with black.

D Click the alpha channel containing the selection to display it in the image window; then paint with white.

4 To view an alpha channel's contents as a colored overlay over the original image, you should:

A Alt+click it.

B Select it and enter Quick Mask mode.

C Select it and view the composite RGB channels at the same time.

D Choose View, Extras.

5 Which key do you press while clicking a layer mask thumbnail in the Layers panel to view the mask in the image window?

A  Alt

B  Ctrl

C  Shift

D  Caps Lock

6 Gray pixels in a layer mask make the corresponding image pixels:

A  More gray

B  Semi-transparent

C  Hard-edged

D  Inverted

7 Name three ways to create gray pixels within a layer mask.

8 Describe the relationship between the Refine Edge dialog box and the Refine Mask dialog box.

9 You can use the Refine Edge dialog box to adjust all of the following settings except:

A  Radius

B  Contrast

C  Feather

D  Tolerance

## Independent practice activity

In this activity, you'll load a selection and then save it as a layer mask. Then you'll edit the mask. You'll also add a type mask to the image. Finally, you'll refine a mask by using the Refine Mask dialog box.

The files for this activity are in Student Data folder **Unit 3\Unit summary**.

1 Open Eagle 1 and save the image as **My eagle 1**.

2 Load the channel **Rough selection** as a selection.

3 On the Eagle layer, create a layer mask from the selection.

4 Using the Brush tool, edit the layer mask to remove as much of the original background as you can, without erasing any detail from the eagle. (*Hint*: Don't spend too much time trying to get as close as possible to the feathers around the eagle's head.)

5 Open the Properties panel. Click **Mask Edge**.

6 Refine the mask edge to eliminate the original background from around the eagle. Click OK when you're finished. (*Hint*: You probably don't want to increase the Radius, since the edges around the eagle are sharp.)

7 If necessary, paint with a soft brush, using black, to eliminate any artifacts around the eagle.

8 Using the Horizontal Type Mask tool, type EAGLE on the Eagle layer with the following formatting: **Arial, Black, 250 pt**. Position the selection as shown in Exhibit 3-6, then commit the edit.

9 Save the selection as a channel named **EAGLE text**.

10 Fill the selection with white, then deselect it. (*Hint*: First, make sure the Eagle layer mask thumbnail is selected.)

11 Update ad close the image.

*Exhibit 3-6: The My eagle 1 image after Step 8 of the Independent practice activity*

# Unit 4

## Vector shapes

Complete this unit, and you'll know how to:

**A** Understand how vector layers differ from raster layers and when you might use a vector layer.

**B** Use the path tools and commands to create vector paths and shapes.

**C** Use the path tools and options to edit vector paths.

**D** Use paths to apply creative effects to type.

# Topic A: Vector layers

This topic covers the following ACE exam objectives for Photoshop CS6.

| # | Objective |
|---|-----------|
| **5.2** | **Understanding the differences between raster and shape layers** |
| 5.2.1 | Understanding vector layers in Photoshop |
| 5.2.2 | Understanding the benefits of vector layers |
| 5.2.3 | Comparing and contrasting raster vs. vector |

## Raster and vector graphics

Most of the images you work with in Photoshop are composed of pixels. A *pixel* is the smallest measurable unit of an image on the screen. An image that is made up of a grid (or raster) of pixels is known as a bitmap or *raster* graphic. Examples of raster graphics include digital photos and scanned material. You can use Photoshop to select and manipulate pixels—or just a single pixel—to change a raster image's appearance either subtly or completely.

By contrast, illustration programs such as Adobe Illustrator create and manipulate *vector* graphics, which are defined by mathematical formulas that generate geometric shapes. Vector graphics are used to create logos and other types of artwork that include discrete geometric objects, rather than photographic images that contain subtle gradations of shades and color.

Vector graphics sometimes resemble raster graphics, but because vector graphics are defined as a series of mathematical instructions (not as a group of pixels), different principles control their appearance and behavior. If you increase the size of a vector graphic, it will still look smooth on screen or in print, as shown in Exhibit 4-1.

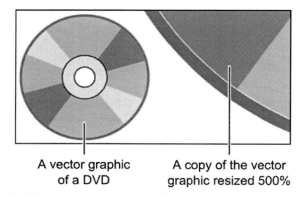

A vector graphic          A copy of the vector
of a DVD                  graphic resized 500%

*Exhibit 4-1: A vector graphic shown at two sizes*

Because a raster graphic contains a specific, fixed number of pixels, increasing its size generally results in increasing the size of its component pixels. This can result in a jagged appearance on screen and in print, as shown in Exhibit 4-2.

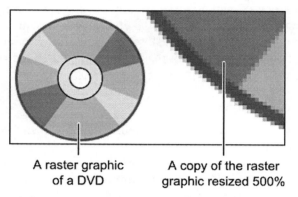

A raster graphic
of a DVD

A copy of the raster
graphic resized 500%

*Exhibit 4-2: A raster graphic shown at two sizes*

Although Photoshop images can include both vector and raster components, Photoshop's environment is designed primarily for manipulating raster components.

*Do it!*

## A-1: Identifying attributes of raster and vector graphics

### Questions and answers

1  True or false? Raster graphics are created from a grid of pixels.

2  True or false? Photographic images are usually made up of vectors.

3  True or false? A Photoshop file can contain both raster and vector components.

4  True or false? A raster image will always print cleanly when scaled to any size.

## Uses for vector paths

*Explanation*

Most images you work with in Photoshop are probably made up entirely of pixels. However, you can also create *vector path*s to define lines and areas geometrically. Purposes for which you would use vector paths might include:

- Selecting and masking image areas that have clearly defined shapes, such as straight lines or smooth curves.
- Creating geometric graphics that are easy to draw and modify.
- Adding *clipping paths* to define transparent areas in an image that you plan to place in another application for print use.
- Flowing text or brush shapes along a path.

### Using vector paths as selection masks and layer masks

When you want to select or mask part of an image that has a geometric shape or is very detailed, you'll often get more accurate results by using vector paths. Additionally, you can scale up vector masks with no loss in quality. You can't directly use a vector path to partially mask image pixels, as you can by painting with gray in an alpha channel, in a pixel-based layer mask, or in Quick Mask mode. However, after creating a path in the shape of the area you want to select or mask, you can convert the vector path to a selection or layer mask.

### Drawing geometric graphics

You can also use vector paths to draw geometric graphics in an image. Using the shape and Pen tools, you can create geometric graphics that are easier to modify and reshape than are pixel-based areas created with the Brush or Pencil tools. When you flatten an image containing shape layers, the image's appearance doesn't change, but the vector paths themselves are removed, leaving only pixels.

### Flowing type or brush shapes along a path

You can also use vector paths as guides for flowing text. For example, you can create text along a curving path. In addition, you can apply a stroke to the path based on a brush shape. The path then looks like it was drawn with the Brush tool.

### Creating clipping paths

You might use Photoshop to create an image for use in another program. However, not all programs will support transparency in the image. To ensure that an image retains transparency when exported to a print application, use a vector path as a clipping path that specifies the visible area, leaving the area outside the clipping path transparent.

*Do it!*

## A-2: Discussing the uses of vector paths

**Questions and answers**

1  In what circumstances might you want to use vector paths to specify an image selection?

2  What is a benefit of drawing with the Pen and shape tools instead of painting with the Brush or Pencil tools?

3  What is the purpose of using a vector path as a clipping path?

# Topic B:  Vector shapes

This topic covers the following ACE exam objectives for Photoshop CS6.

| # | Objective |
|---|-----------|
| **8.2** | **Using vector shapes** |
| 8.2.1 | Creating and modifying vector shapes |
| 8.2.2 | Modifying stroke and fill |
| 8.2.3 | Creating pen-based shapes |
| 8.2.4 | Stroking a path |
| 8.2.5 | Appending and inserting custom shapes |

## The Freeform Pen tool

*Explanation*

The *Pen tools* and *path editing tools* are stored in the group that shows the Pen tool by default, as shown in Exhibit 4-3. They include the Freeform Pen tool, which you can use to draw paths of any shape, much as you can use the Lasso tool to create selections of any shape. When you select the Freeform Pen tool, the options bar displays the options shown in Exhibit 4-4.

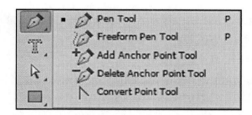

*Exhibit 4-3: The pen and path editing tools*

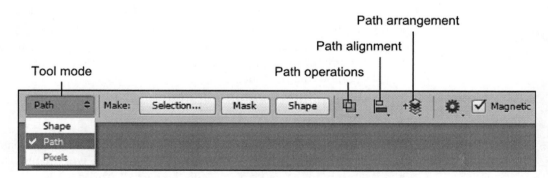

*Exhibit 4-4: Some of the Freeform Pen tool options on the options bar*

Several of the Freeform Pen tool options are described in the following table.

| Item | Description |
| --- | --- |
| Tool modes | From the list, select Shape if you want the paths you create to generate *shape layers*. You can use a shape layer to add shapes filled with the current foreground color or filled with a style that applies a gradient or pattern.<br><br>Select Path if you want the paths you create to generate *work paths*. You can use work paths to create vector paths that make no visible change in the image but can be used to create selections or clipping paths. |
| Path operations | By selecting an option from this list, you can combine, subtract from, merge, or exclude overlapping paths you create. |
| Path alignment | By selecting an option from this list, you can align path edges or centers, or you can distribute paths. |
| Path arrangement | By selecting an option from this list, you can adjust the stacking order of paths in an image. |
| Magnetic | Similar to the Magnetic Lasso tool, this setting makes the path you create snap to contrasting areas of the image based on settings you specify by clicking the gear icon to the left. |

To use the Freeform Pen tool to draw a freeform vector path with the Magnetic option:

1. Select the Freeform Pen tool.
2. On the options bar, check Magnetic.
3. Point to where you want to begin the path, and click to add the first *fastening point*, which indicates where the path begins.
4. Move the pointer within the image to specify the shape of the path. As you move the pointer, fastening points appear along the path to specify where it flows. You can click to add a fastening point where you want one, and you can press Backspace or Delete to remove the last fastening point added.
5. Point to the first fastening point (where you started the path), and when the pointer displays a small circle, click to close the path. You can also double-click at any time to complete the path with a segment connecting the last fastening point to the first one.

## Saving paths

When you create a path with the Paths option selected on the options bar, the new path is added as a work path, as shown in Exhibit 4-5. The work path is visible in the image, and it appears in the Paths panel with the name "Work Path."

The work path you've created is temporary. If you click a blank part of the Paths panel to deselect the work path and then draw a new path, the new one will replace the old one. However, you can save a work path as a permanent path:

1. In the Paths panel, double-click Work Path to open the Save Path dialog box.
2. In the Name box, enter a name for the path.
3. Click OK.

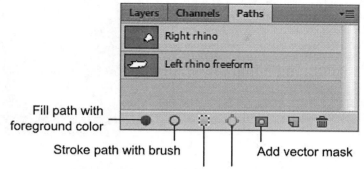

Fill path with foreground color

Stroke path with brush

Load path as a selection

Make work path from selection

Add vector mask

*Exhibit 4-5: The Paths panel*

*Do it!*

## B-1: Creating a freeform path

The files for this activity are in Student Data folder **Unit 4\Topic B**.

| Here's how | Here's why |
|---|---|
| 1 Open Rhinos 3 | |
| Save the image as **My rhinos 3** | (In the current topic folder.) You'll use the Freeform Pen tool to draw a path that traces the outline of the left rhino. |
| 2 In the Tools panel, click and hold | To display the Pen tools. |
| Select the **Freeform Pen Tool** | |
| On the options bar, verify that Path is selected | To specify that the paths you draw will generate work paths, rather than shape layers. |
| On the options bar, check **Magnetic** | To snap the path to contrasting areas in the image. A small horseshoe magnet is added to the pointer icon. |
| 3 Click the tip of the left rhino's horn, as shown | To place the first fastening point, which determines where the path begins. |

4 Move the pointer across the rhino's horn to the right

Additional fastening points appear along the path as you move the pointer. With the default settings, however, the Freeform Pen tool doesn't flow exactly where you want it to.

5 Press (← BACKSPACE)

(As necessary.) To remove previous fastening points.

Click as shown

To manually add a fastening point.

6 Continue drawing a path across the rhino's back

Add and delete fastening points as necessary.

Draw a path around only the left rhino

Where the two rhinos meet, trace the path around the right rhino so that you don't include it in the path.

7 When the pointer is over the initial fastening point, click the mouse

(Point to the initial fastening point, and when the pointer displays a small circle, click.) To close the path.

8 Click the **Paths** panel

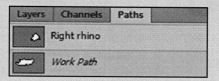

The image already includes a path that was saved previously. The path you just created appears as Work Path. You'll save the work path.

Double-click **Work Path**                    To open the Save Path dialog box.

Edit the Name box to read **Left rhino freeform**

Click **OK**                    To save the path.

9 Click a blank area in the Paths panel                    To deselect the path. It's no longer visible in the image window.

10 Update the image

## Converting selections to paths

*Explanation*

Another way to create a path is to convert a selection to a path. This method is particularly useful when you want to generate a path for an item that you can easily select with the selection tools.

To convert a selection to a path, click the "Make work path from selection" button in the Paths panel. The new path is created with the default settings. If you want to control how accurately the path matches the shape of the original selection, then before you convert the selection to a path, change settings in the Make Work Path dialog box.

To open the Make Work Path dialog box, do either of the following:

- From the Paths panel menu, choose Make Work Path.
- Press Alt and click the "Make work path from selection" button.

In the Make Work Path dialog box, you can specify a Tolerance value. The lower the tolerance, the more closely the path will match the shape of the original selection. In addition, a lower tolerance will generate a path with more anchor points. A higher tolerance will generate a smoother path with fewer anchor points, but the path won't conform as closely to the original shape of the selection.

*Do it!* **B-2: Converting a selection to a path**

| Here's how | Here's why |
|---|---|
| 1 Click the **Channels** panel | |
| Press ⌈CTRL⌋ and click the **Rhinos** channel | To make it a selection. |
| 2 In the Paths panel, press ⌈ALT⌋ and click ◇ | (The "Make work path from selection" button.) To open the Make Work Path dialog box. The default Tolerance value is 2.0. |
| Click **OK** | To create a path from the selection you just made. |
| 3 Double-click **Work Path** | To open the Save Path dialog box. |
| Name the path **Rhinos from selection 2px** | Double-click the path name, edit the Name box, and click OK. |
| 4 In the Tools panel, click ▶ | (The Path Selection tool.) You can use the Path Selection tool to select and manipulate a path. |
| In the image window, click the path | To observe the number of points and the accuracy and smoothness of the path. |
| | You'll deselect the path and create a second, more accurate path. |
| Deselect the path | In the Paths panel, click a blank area below the path. |
| 5 Choose **Select, Reselect** | To select the most recent selection. |
| In the Paths panel, press ⌈ALT⌋ and click ◇ | |
| Edit the Tolerance box to read **1** | To specify that the path uses more anchor points. |
| Click **OK** | To create the work path. |
| Name the work path **Rhinos from selection 1px** | |
| 6 Using the Path Selection tool, select the path you just created | Observe that the path is more accurate, but contains more anchor points. |
| Deselect the path | Click a blank area of the Paths panel. |
| 7 Update the image | |

## The Pen tool

*Explanation*    Another way to create a path is to use the Pen tool. When you use the Pen tool to create a path, you have more control over the path's shape than you do with other methods. With the Pen tool, you specify the location of anchor points and direction points to create straight or curving segments with precision.

## Path components

Paths created in Photoshop are made up of anchor points, segments, and direction points, as shown in Exhibit 4-6. The *anchor points* determine where the path flows. A *segment* is the part of a path between two anchor points. *Direction points* determine the curvature (if any) of each segment.

Direction points extend from anchor points. Each anchor point can have two direction points, with each one controlling the curvature of the segment on either side of the anchor point. If a segment contains no curvature, its anchor points won't have associated direction points.

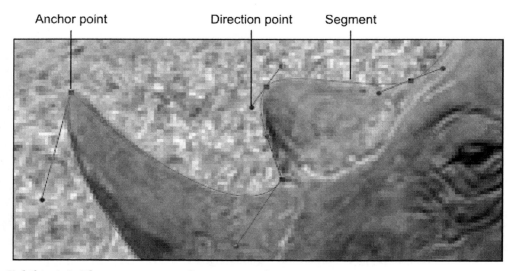

*Exhibit 4-6: The components of a vector path*

### Selecting paths and path components

The *selection tools* are stored in the group that shows the Path Selection tool by default. The technique you use to select a path depends on what you want to do with it:

- To show a path in the image window, click the path in the Paths panel. You can then create a selection from the path, apply or adjust a fill or stroke, and more. To hide any paths in the image, click a blank area of the Paths panel.
- To display a path's anchor points, click the path with the Path Selection tool. You can then drag the path to move it.
- To display a path's associated direction points, click a segment or anchor point with the Direct Selection tool. You can then drag direction points and anchor points to reshape the path.

### Straight segments

To create a straight segment, with the Pen tool, click to place two anchor points, as shown in Exhibit 4-7. A straight segment appears between the two anchor points, and there are no direction points. You can continue clicking to add more segments to the path.

To begin a new path, press Esc or click the Pen tool in the Tools panel. A small "×" appears next to the Pen tool's pointer when it's ready to begin a new path. To draw a horizontal, vertical, or 45-degree segment, press Shift as you click to add the second anchor point.

*Exhibit 4-7: A straight segment connecting two anchor points*

### Curving segments

To create a curving segment, point to where you want to begin the path. Click and drag in the direction you want the path to curve. Point to where you want to add the second anchor point, and drag in the direction you want the path to move as it enters the second anchor point.

For example, to create a rainbow shape, drag up to indicate that the path should curve upward from the first anchor point, as shown in Exhibit 4-8. Point to where you want to place the second anchor point, and drag down to indicate that the path should curve downward as it enters that anchor point, as shown in Exhibit 4-9.

*Exhibit 4-8: The first anchor point and direction point for a curving segment*

*Exhibit 4-9: A curving segment*

### Smooth points and corner points

When you drag to create an anchor point with a direction point, a second direction point is created to control the curvature of the next segment. By default, the next segment will continue the first segment's curve direction. So if a segment curves downward into its second anchor point, the path will continue to curve downward as it leaves that anchor point for the next segment. When the segments on either side of an anchor point curve in the same direction, that anchor point is called a *smooth point*, shown in Exhibit 4-10.

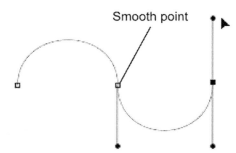

*Exhibit 4-10: Two segments connected by a smooth point*

You can specify a different direction for the second segment, thereby creating a *corner point*. To draw a path's second segment with a corner point, press Alt to temporarily select the Convert Point tool, and drag the existing direction point for the next segment to specify the direction you want the next segment to curve in, as shown in Exhibit 4-11.

You can then release Alt to return to the Pen tool, and drag to specify the ending anchor point and direction point for the segment, as shown in Exhibit 4-12. Dragging a direction point with the Convert Point tool converts a smooth point to a corner point. You can do this while drawing a path or after a path is complete.

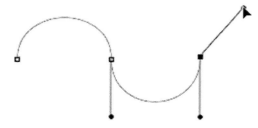

*Exhibit 4-11: Dragging a direction point with the Convert Point tool to specify a corner point*

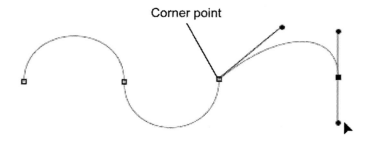

*Exhibit 4-12: Two segments connected by a corner point*

If you click twice to create a straight segment, you can drag from the second anchor point to create a single direction point to specify the curvature for the next segment, without affecting the existing straight segment.

In addition, if you want to draw a straight segment following a curving segment, you can press Alt and click the curving segment's second anchor point to remove the direction point that would have applied curvature to the following segment. The existing curving segment won't be affected.

*Do it!*

## B-3: Creating paths with the Pen tool

| Here's how | Here's why |
|---|---|
| 1 In the Paths panel, press `ALT` and click 🔲 | (The Create new path button.) To open the New Path dialog box. |
| Name the path **Left rhino pen** | |
| Click **OK** | To create a new path. |
| 2 Zoom to 300% on the left rhino's head | You'll begin drawing a path around the rhino's horn. |
| 3 Right-click the Freeform Pen tool and select the **Pen Tool** | |
| 4 Click as shown | To place the first anchor point at the tip of the left rhino's horn. |
| 5 Click and hold as shown | Hold the mouse button down. |

6  Drag up and to the right, as
   shown, and then release the
   mouse

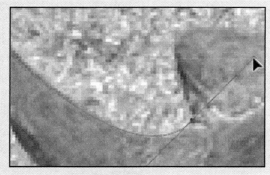

To create the curved segment along the horn.

7  Press ( ALT ) and drag the right
   direction point for the anchor
   point you just created, as shown

To allow the right direction point to move at an
independent angle, letting you create a sharp
corner.

8  Click and drag as shown

To create another curved segment.

9  Click and drag as shown

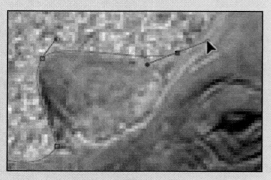

To create a curved segment around the rhino's
smaller horn..

10  Update the image

## Shape layers

*Explanation*

You can also use vector paths to draw geometric graphics in an image. You can use Photoshop's shape tools or Pen tools to draw a shape, so that a new shape layer is created automatically. The shape tools are stored in the group that shows the Rectangle tool by default, as shown in Exhibit 4-13.

A *shape layer* is actually a solid fill layer with a vector mask. Creating shapes by using a shape layer is useful when you want to be able to easily edit and scale the shape with path editing tools.

When you select a shape tool, on the options bar, Shape is selected by default from the Pick tool mode list. Drawing with a shape tool in Shape mode creates a shape (that is, a fill layer and a vector mask) on a new layer. However, you can select Path from the Pick tool mode list to draw a path from the shape instead. Likewise, you can use a pen tool to create a shape layer, meaning you have endless possibilities for creating custom shapes.

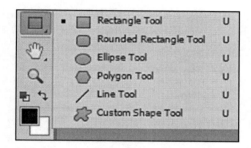

*Exhibit 4-13: The shape tools*

Photoshop includes a number of custom shapes in addition to the ones shown by default in the Custom Shape picker on the options bar. To replace the current set or append a new set of shapes to it, open the Custom Shape picker and click the gear icon, shown in Exhibit 4-14. When you select a set of shapes, a warning box appears, asking whether you want to replace the current shapes. To do so, click OK; to add the new shapes to the current ones, click Append.

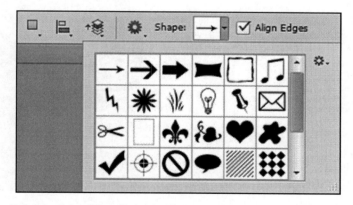

*Exhibit 4-14: The Custom Shape picker*

*Do it!*

## B-4:    Creating a vector shape layer

| Here's how | Here's why |
|---|---|
| 1  Fit the image in the window | |
| 2  In the Layers panel, select the **Rhinos** layer | |
| 3  In the Tools panel, right-click ▣ and select the **Custom Shape Tool** | |
| 4  On the options bar, click as shown | To open the Custom Shape picker. |
| Click ⚙. | To show options for working with custom shapes. |
| Choose **Frames** | A warning box appears. |
| Click **Append** | To add the Frames shapes to the current custom shapes. |
| 5  In the Custom Shape picker, scroll down | To see the Frames shapes. |
| Select the indicated shape | The Frame 7 shape. |
| 6  Create a frame shape in the image, as shown | |
| 7  Double-click the **Shape 1** layer | To open the Layer Style dialog box. |
| Under Styles, click **Color Overlay** | To display the Color Overlay settings. |
| Select a light gray color | |
| Click **Inner Shadow** | To use the default settings for the layer style. |
| Click **OK** | To close the Layer Style dialog box. |

8 Name the layer **Frame**

9 In the Layers panel, click below    To deselect the shape layer.
  the last layer

10 Update the image

## Applying strokes and fills to paths and shapes

*Explanation*

Another way to use a path as an artistic element in an image is to create a brush stroke based on the path's shape or to fill the path with a color. When you create a brush stroke based on a path, the stroke follows the shape of all paths and subpaths, regardless of the options you specified for how the subpaths interact.

If a path includes overlapping subpaths, and you want to apply a brush stroke to only the outer border of the overlapping paths, you should first combine the overlapping subpaths into a single path.

### Applying a brush stroke to paths

To apply a brush stroke to a path:

1 In the Paths panel, select the path you want to stroke. If the path includes overlapping subpaths that you want to combine, then follow these steps:

  a If you want to keep a copy of the original path with the subpaths, drag the path to the Create new path button in the Paths panel to make a copy.

  b In the duplicate path, use the Path Selection tool to select each subpath you want to combine.

  c On the options bar, click Combine.

2 In the Layers panel, select the layer that you want the stroke to appear on.

3 In the Tools panel, select the Brush tool.

4 In the Brush Preset picker, select the brush you want to use.

5 In the Paths panel, click the "Stroke path with brush" button.

### Stroking and filling shapes

The stroke and fill options for a shape layer appear on the options bar when a shape tool is selected. To apply or modify a shape's stroke and fill, select the shape layer and then select a shape tool. Then, on the options bar, select options as shown in Exhibit 4-15.

*Exhibit 4-15: Shape tool stroke and fill options*

*Do it!*

## B-5: Stroking a path with a brush shape

| Here's how | Here's why |
|---|---|
| 1 In the Layers panel, create a new layer at the top of the stacking order named **Rhinos stroke** | |
| 2 In the Paths panel, select **Rhinos from selection 1 px** | |
| 3 Set the foreground color to a green color | |
| 4 Using the Path Selection tool, select the path | In the image. |
| In the Paths panel, click [ ◯ ] | (The Stroke path with brush button.) To apply a green stroke to the path. |
| 5 Select the Brush tool | |
| In the Brush Preset picker, select the indicated brush | |

The Spatter 14 pixels brush.

| Here's how | Here's why |
|---|---|
| In the Paths panel, click [ ◯ ] | To modify the stroke. |
| 6 In the Layers panel, select the **Frame** layer | |
| 7 Select the Custom Shape tool | |
| On the options bar, click as shown | |

| | |
|---|---|
| | To display the options for modifying the shape's stroke. By default, the shape is set to No Color. |
| Click [ ■ ] | To stroke the shape with a solid color. |
| Click a green color swatch | To modify the shape's stroke color. |
| 8 Select the **Rhinos stroke** layer | |
| Set the Opacity to **40%** | |
| 9 Click below the last layer | To deselect all layers. |
| 10 Update and close the image | |

# Topic C:   Editing vector paths

*Explanation*

After creating a path, you can change its shape. You can add and remove anchor points and direction points, convert smooth points to corner points, and drag segments, anchor points, and direction points.

## The Direct Selection tool

To modify a path, you can use the Direct Selection tool and the following techniques:

- Drag a curving segment to increase or decrease its curvature without changing the angle of the direction points.
- Drag a direction point to adjust the curvature of its associated segment.
- Drag an anchor point to move it; this adjusts the segments on either side of the anchor point.

When you drag a direction point attached to a smooth point, the other direction point connected to the anchor point moves as well. To move a direction point independently, use the Convert Point tool to drag it. When you use the Convert Point tool to drag a direction point, you convert the smooth point to a corner point.

## Adding and removing anchor points

After completing a path, you can add or remove anchor points. To add a point, you can select the Pen tool or the Add Anchor Point tool, point to any path segment, and click. When you use the Pen tool to point to a path segment, the pointer displays a plus sign (+), indicating that clicking will add an anchor point.

You can remove an anchor point by using either the Pen tool or the Delete Anchor Point tool; just point to the anchor point and click. When you use the Pen tool to point to an anchor point, the mouse pointer displays a minus sign (–), indicating that clicking will delete the anchor point.

*Do it!*

### C-1:   Adjusting path points

The files for this activity are in Student Data folder **Unit 4\Topic C**.

| Here's how | Here's why |
|---|---|
| 1  Open Rhinos 4 | |
|    Save the image as **My rhinos 4** | In the current topic folder. |
| 2  Zoom to 300% on the left rhino's head | |
| 3  In the Tools panel, right-click the Path Selection tool and select the **Direct Selection Tool** | You'll drag segments, anchor points, and direction points to adjust the path's shape. |
| 4  In the Paths panel, select **Rhinos from selection 1 px** | To activate the path in the image. |
|    Click the path | To select it and view the anchor points. |

5 Drag the indicated anchor point as shown

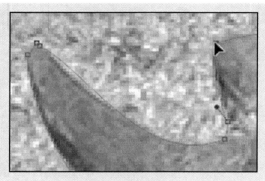

To move it slightly inside the boundary between the background and the rhino's second horn. This point is a corner point; you'll convert it to a smooth point.

6 Right-click the Pen tool group and select the **Convert Point Tool**

Click the point you just dragged and drag up and to the right slightly

To convert the point and adjust the direction handles.

7 Drag the indicated segment closer to the rhino's horn

When you move the segment, the anchor points on either end remain fixed, but their direction handles adjust automatically.

8  Scroll to the left rhino's front feet

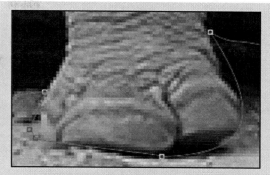

The path doesn't match the rhino's left foot very well. You'll add anchor points to give you more control over the path.

9  Using the Pen tool, click as shown

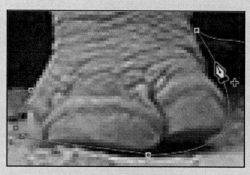

To add another anchor point to the curve.

Hold CTRL

To temporarily select the Direct Selection tool.

Drag the anchor point closer to the rhino's foot

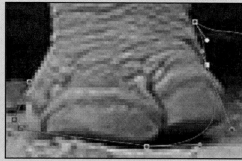

10  Create additional anchor points and position them as shown

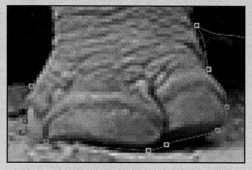

Adjust anchor point positions and direction handles as necessary.

11  Update the image

## Subpaths

*Explanation*
When a path is selected in the Paths panel, any new paths you create are added as *subpaths*. Creating subpaths is useful when you want to use paths to generate a selection or create a mask made up of more than one area or shape. When you create subpaths, you can select options from the Path operations list on the options bar, shown in Exhibit 4-16, to specify how the paths will interact with each other where they overlap.

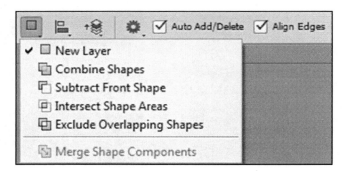

*Exhibit 4-16: Path operations options for combining subpaths*

The options for combining subpaths are described in the following table.

| Button | Description |
| --- | --- |
| Combine Shapes | The area within new subpaths you draw is added to the original path. A selection or mask generated from the paths includes the area within all of the paths. |
| Subtract Front Shape | New subpaths you draw remove any part of the original path that they overlap. A selection or mask generated from the paths includes only the area of the original path that's not overlapped by any of the subpaths. |
| Intersect Shape Areas | A new subpath you draw restricts the path to the area where it intersects with the original path. A selection or mask generated from the paths includes only the area where they intersect. |
| Exclude Overlapping Shapes | A new subpath you draw is added to the path area, but overlapping areas are removed. A selection or mask generated from the paths includes the area within all paths, except for the areas where they overlap. |

After creating a path, you can apply a different path operation to it. To do so, use the Path Selection tool to select the subpath, and select the path operation you want.

### Converting paths to selections

You can convert a path in the Paths panel to a selection by using either of these techniques:

- Select the path in the Paths panel and then click the "Load path as a selection" button.
- Press Ctrl and click the path in the Paths panel.

*Do it!*  ### C-2: Combining subpaths

| Here's how | Here's why |
|---|---|
| 1  In the Layers panel, select the **Text shadow** layer | |
| Select the Magic Wand tool | |
| On the options bar, clear **Contiguous** | |
| In the image, click one of the letters in the word RHINOS | To select the letter shapes on the layer. |
| 2  In the Paths panel, click ⬦ | |
| Save the work path as RHINOS | Double-click it and edit the Name box, then click OK. |
| 3  Using the Path Selection tool, click the path around the letter R | When you converted from a selection, each distinct selection became a separate path. You'll merge them. |
| On the options bar, from the Path operations list, select **Merge Shape Components** | |
| Click the path around the R again | This time, all of the shapes in the path are selected. |
| 4  Press CTRL + C | To copy the path. |
| 5  In the Layers panel, create a new layer at the top of the stacking order named **Path operations** | You'll experiment with different path operations to combine the path around the rhinos with the path you created from the text. |
| 6  In the Paths panel, select the **Rhinos from selection 1 px** path | |
| Press D | |
| Click ● | To fill the path with a black color. |

7 Press (CTRL) + (V)      To paste the shapes you copied into the selected path.

Using the Path Selection tool, move the letter shapes to the indicated position

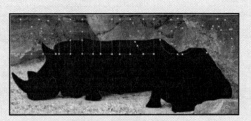

So that the shapes overlap.

Press (CTRL) and click the path around the rhinos      To select both shapes.

8 Press (X)

9 On the options bar, from the Path operations list, select
**Combine Shapes**

Click ⦿      To fill both paths with the foreground color.

Press (CTRL) + (Z)

10 On the options bar, from the Path operations list, select
**Subtract Front Shape**

Click ⦿

Press (CTRL) + (Z)

11 On the options bar, from the Path operations list, select
**Intersect Shape Areas**

Click ⦿

Press (CTRL) + (Z)

12 On the options bar, from the Path operations list, select
**Exclude Overlapping Shapes**

Click ⦿

13 Update and close the image

# Topic D:  Vector paths and type

*Explanation*    In addition to creating paths as clipping paths, as masks, or for generating selections, you can use vector paths to work with type. For example, you can adjust the shape of text characters and create a path on which to flow text.

## Converting type to paths

The font files you use to create text define each character as a vector path. Ordinarily, you don't see or adjust the points and path segments, but they're used to generate the shapes with smooth edges at any size. Photoshop allows you to convert type layers back to the original vector paths, which you can then adjust to change the character shapes, as shown in Exhibit 4-17.

To convert type to a path:

1   Select the type layer.
2   Either right-click the type layer or choose Layer, Type. Then choose a command to convert the type:

- If you want to replace the type layer with a shape layer that looks identical (but has editable path shapes), choose Convert to Shape.
- If you want the type layer to remain, and you want to add the path outlines to the Paths panel as the work path, choose Create Work Path.

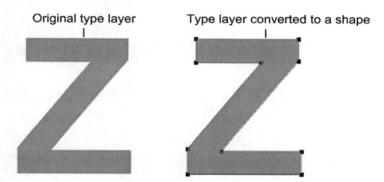

Original type layer          Type layer converted to a shape

*Exhibit 4-17: Type converted to a shape*

*Do it!*

### D-1: Converting type characters to editable shapes

The files for this activity are in Student Data folder **Unit 4\Topic D**.

| Here's how | Here's why |
|---|---|
| 1 Open Rhino ad 1 | |
| Save the image as **My rhino ad 1** | (In the current topic folder.) You'll extend the bottom-right side of the "k" in "Park" to the right edge of the image. First, you'll duplicate the layer to retain the original version. |
| 2 Drag the **Pangaea Zoo** layer to the "Create a new layer" icon | |
| Hide the Pangaea Zoo layer | You can revert to this layer later, if necessary. |
| 3 Right-click the **Pangaea Zoo copy** layer and choose **Convert to Shape** | To convert the type to a shape layer with a vector mask in the shape of the text characters. |
| 4 Using the Direct Selection tool, click the **Z** at the beginning of "Zoological" | |
| | You'll adjust the anchor points in order to extend the bottom of the character to the right. |
| Click the indicated anchor point | |
| Hold (SHIFT) and click the indicated anchor point | To select the two anchor points at the bottom-right of the Z. Don't release Shift yet. |

5  Drag the anchor point to the right
   edge of the image, as shown

6  Select the Path Selection tool

   Press ⸤CTRL⸥ + ⸤X⸥          To cut the Z shape from the path. You'll paste it
                              on its own path.

7  In the Layers panel, create a new
   layer named **Z**

   Move the Z layer below the
   Pangaea Zoo copy layer

   Press ⸤CTRL⸥ + ⸤V⸥          To paste the Z shape.

8  In the Paths panel, click ⸤✳⸥    The Load path as a selection button.

   Set the foreground color to orange

   Press ⸤ALT⸥ + ⸤← BACKSPACE⸥   To fill the selection with orange.

   Deselect the selection

9  Press ⸤CTRL⸥ + ⸤T⸥

   Scale and position the path as
   shown

10  Right-click the Pangaea Zoo
    copy layer

    Choose **Copy Layer Style**

    Right-click the Z layer

    Choose **Paste Layer Style**

11  Update the image

### Type on a path

*Explanation*

To add text that flows along a path:

1   In the Tools panel, select a Type tool.
2   In the Paths panel, select the path you want the text to flow along.
3   In the image window, click the path at the location where you want to begin adding text. A flashing insertion point appears. A new type layer appears in the Layers panel. A new type path appears in the Paths panel, containing a copy of the original path you clicked.
4   Specify the text formatting you want on the options bar, and type to add the text that will flow along the path.

You can also click within a closed path to add type that flows within the path.

*Do it!*

### D-2:   Wrapping type on a path

| Here's how | Here's why |
|---|---|
| 1   In the Paths panel, select **Left rhino freeform** | |
| 2   Using the Horizontal Type tool, click the indicated section of the path | |
| | |
| On the options bar, set the type to **Arial, Bold, 24 pt** | |
| Type **See our new rhino habitat!** | You'll move the type to the left along the path. |
| 3   Select the Path Selection tool | |
| Click the path containing the text | |
| Point to the beginning of the text | |
| | The pointer indicates that you can drag the type to move it. |
| Drag to the left as shown | As you drag, Photoshop resizes the type path. |
| | |

4  Point to the end of the text

Drag to the right

To increase the size of the type path.

5  Select the Move tool

Press ⬆ three times                    To nudge the text up 3 pixels.

6  Deselect the path

7  Update and close the image

# Unit summary: Vector shapes

*Topic A*     In this topic, you learned about the benefits of using **vector layers** and how vector layers differ from raster layers. You also learned about the uses of **vector paths** in Photoshop.

*Topic B*     In this topic, you learned how to use the **Pen tools** to draw paths, and you **converted selections to paths**. You also **saved paths** by using the Paths panel. In addition, you added **vector shapes** to an image. Finally, you created **brush strokes** that flowed along the shape of a path.

*Topic C*     In this topic, you used the Direct Selection tool to **edit paths** by adjusting anchor points, direction points, and segments. You also added and removed anchor points, and you created **subpaths**.

*Topic D*     In this topic, you **converted type to paths** and wrapped type along a path.

## Review questions

1  Which tool cannot directly create a vector path?

   A  Pen                          C  Custom Shape

   B  Rectangle                    D  Lasso

2  How can you create a shape layer that displays an oval filled with a solid color?

   A  Select the Elliptical Marquee tool and drag in the image.

   B  Select the Ellipse tool and drag in the image.

   C  Select the Lasso tool and drag in the image.

   D  Create a new layer; then select the Elliptical Marquee tool and drag in the image.

3  True or false? A vector path must pass through each direction point.


4  To choose exactly where anchor and direction points will be placed along a vector path as you create it, which tool should you use?

   A  The Ellipse tool               C  The Polygon tool

   B  The Lasso tool                 D  The Pen tool

5  Which of the following are advantages of using vector drawing tools versus using raster drawing tools? [Choose all that apply.]

   A  You can add or remove selected areas in Quick Mask mode.

   B  You can select and mask image areas that have clearly defined shapes, such as smoothly flowing curves.

   C  You can create paths in the Paths panel that store semi-transparency information.

   D  You can create geometric graphics that are easy to draw and modify.

6  You want to create a solid-colored geometric object whose shape you can easily modify later. Which type of tools should you use to create the shape?

   A  Vector drawing tools           C  Raster drawing tools

   B  Selection tools                D  Pixel-based drawing tools

7  A path's _____ points determine the curvature of its segments.

8  True or false? A path that appears in the Paths panel might contain a secondary path called a subpath.

9  To hide parts of a layer with a vector path, as you would with a layer mask, what should you create?

10  True or false? "Vector mask" and "clipping path" are interchangeable terms.

11  Name three ways to use vector paths that appear directly in the image, not just in the Paths panel.

12  You want to flow type along a curving path. What should you do?

   A  Use a Path Type tool.

   B  Select the path in the Paths panel, and click with a Type tool at the location where you want to begin adding type.

   C  Select a type layer and a shape layer; then choose Layer, Bind Type to Path.

   D  You can't flow type along a vector path in Photoshop.

13  You're creating a logo based on type you've entered with the Type tool. You want to use the Direct Selection tool to reshape the characters to add visual interest. What must you do to the type layer before you can reshape the letters with the Direct Selection tool?

   A  Choose Layer, Type, Convert to Shape.

   B  Choose Layer, Rasterize, Type.

   C  Choose Layer, New Layer Based Slice.

   D  Choose Layer, Type, Warp Text.

14  How can you save a work path as a permanent path?

   A  Create a selection with any selection tool; then choose Make Work Path from the Paths panel menu.

   B  In the Paths panel, select the work path and click the "Load path as a selection" icon.

   C  In the Paths panel, double-click the work path; then enter a new name and click OK.

   D  In the Paths panel, select the work path and click the "Fill path with foreground color" button.

15 How can you convert a selection to a path?

    A Choose Select, Save Selection.

    B Choose Select, Load Selection.

    C In the Paths panel, click the "Load path as a selection" icon.

    D In the Paths panel, click the "Make work path from selection" icon.

## Independent practice activity

In this activity, you'll create a path. Then you'll adjust the path. You'll also apply a stroke to the path. In addition, you'll wrap text along a path. Finally, you'll add a custom shape to the image.

The files for this activity are in Student Data folder **Unit 4\Unit summary**.

1 Open Lion 1 and save the image as **My lion 1**.

2 Using one of the techniques you've learned, create a path around the lion. Save it as a path named **Lion**. (*Hint*: Either use a Pen tool or make a selection and then convert it to a path.)

3 Adjust the path so that it follows the outline of the lion as closely as possible.

4 Apply a 36-px Chalk brush stroke to the path, using the same color as is used in the text "pangaea."

5 Add the text "zoological park" to the image so that it flows along the lion's back, as shown in Exhibit 4-18. (*Hint*: Use the path you created.)

6 Add the Starburst custom shape to the image. Move the shape layer below the Lion layer.

7 Scale and position the shape layer as shown in Exhibit 4-18.

8 Update and close the image.

*Exhibit 4-18: The image as it appears after Step 7 of the independent practice activity*

# **Unit 5**

## Creative image effects

Complete this unit, and you'll know how to:

**A** Warp text and layers.

**B** Use the Liquify filter to modify an image's pixels.

**C** Use the Black & White options to maximize image contrast when you convert an image to grayscale, and convert a grayscale image to a duotone.

**D** Apply filters as Smart Filters, and mask Smart Filters.

# Topic A: Warping

This topic covers the following ACE exam objectives for Photoshop CS6.

| # | Objective |
|---|-----------|
| **7.4** | **Using Puppet Warp** |
| 7.4.1 | Using the Puppet Warp tool to correct image problems in people and landscape-based images |
| 7.4.2 | Understanding how to add/removal points |
| 7.4.3 | Understanding the increase/decrease of mesh for maximum effective use |

## Warping text and images

*Explanation*

You can reshape text, layer content, or selections by applying a *warp*. You can warp items to apply a variety of creative effects.

## Warping text

You can warp Photoshop text to reshape it for a variety of effects. Warping text reshapes the text characters and flows the text along a curving baseline. After you apply a warp, the text remains editable as text.

To warp text:

1 In the Layers panel, select the type layer.
2 Select either the Horizontal or Vertical Type tool.
3 On the options bar, click the Create warped text button to open the Warp Text dialog box.
4 From the Style list, select a warp style to preview its effect on the text on the selected layer. You can press Down Arrow to select each warp style in the list.
5 Select Horizontal or Vertical to specify the direction in which the style will affect the text.
6 Specify Bend, Horizontal Distortion, and Vertical Distortion values to control how the warp style will affect the text.
7 Click OK.

*Do it!*     **A-1: Warping text**

The files for this activity are in Student Data folder **Unit 5\Topic A**.

| Here's how | Here's why |
|---|---|
| 1  Open Background 4 | |
| Save the image as **My background 4** | In the current topic folder. |
| 2  Select the **NECTARINES** layer | If necessary. |
| 3  Select the Horizontal Type tool | |
| On the options bar, click [icon] | (The Create warped text button.) To open the Warp Text dialog box. |
| 4  From the Style list, select **Arc** | |
| Observe the text in the image | The text now flows along a curved baseline. |
| Press ⬇ several times | To view each style. |
| 5  From the Style list, select **Fish** | |
| Set the Bend value to **-50** | |
| Set the Horizontal Distortion value to **-40** | |
| Set the Vertical Distortion value to **0** | If necessary. |
| 6  Click **OK** | |

## Warping images

*Explanation*

You can also warp image content. You can warp a selection or an entire layer by applying a preset warp or creating a custom warp.

To warp a selection or layer:

1 Create a selection, or select a layer in the Layers panel. (To select a layer, you can click it in the Layers panel, or press Ctrl and click any of the layer's content in the image window.)

2 Choose Edit, Transform, Warp to add a warp grid to the selection or layer.

3 Apply a preset warp, a custom warp, or both.

- Drag the grid handles to warp the selection.

- On the options bar, select a preset warp from the Warp list. To further customize the preset warp effect, select Custom from the Warp list and drag the grid handles.

4 Press Enter to apply the warp.

You can use the Edit, Transform, Warp command and the Warp list on the options bar to apply a preset warp to a type layer. However, you can't apply a custom warp to a type layer.

*Do it!*    ## A-2:   Warping image layers

| Here's how | Here's why |
|---|---|
| 1  Select the **Circles** layer | |
|    Press (CTRL) + (ALT) + (J) | To duplicate the layer and open the New Layer dialog box. |
|    Name the layer **Circles warped** | |
|    Hide the Circles layer | |
| 2  Choose **Edit**, **Transform**, **Warp** | A warp grid appears on the circles. |
|    On the options bar, from the Warp list, select **Arc** | |
|    Press (↓) several times | To view each style. |
| 3  From the Warp list, select **Inflate** | |
|    From the Warp list, select **Custom** | To customize the Inflate warp style. |
| 4  Drag the bottom-right handle of the grid down, as shown |  X : 6.736 in  Y : 8.696 in |
| | To adjust the curvature. |

5 Point within the grid

Notice that the mouse pointer changes shape.

Drag the indicated area down and to the right, as shown

To further distort the image.

6 Drag the direction handle extending from the top-right corner of the warp mesh as shown

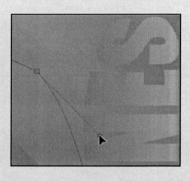

7 Press (↵ ENTER)

To complete the warp.

8 Choose **Edit**, **Transform**, **Warp**

A grid with even squares appears. You can't access a warp's original grid or clear an image warp after committing it.

Press (ESC)

To clear the grid.

9 Update and close the image

## Puppet Warp

*Explanation*

Another tool you can use to warp an image with even more control is the Puppet Warp command. Using this command, you can transform and distort image areas while leaving other parts of the image intact. For example, you can use Puppet Warp to straighten a curved road or to rotate a subject's arm or leg while leaving the rest of the body unmoved.

To use Puppet Warp:

1  Select the layer containing the object you want to warp.

2  Choose Edit, Puppet Warp. A mesh appears over the contents of the layer.

3  On the options bar, select the desired settings, as shown in Exhibit 5-1:

   • **Mode** — Determines the overall elasticity of the mesh.

   • **Density** — Determines the spacing of the mesh. For more precise warping, select More Points, but be aware that this can increase processing time.

   • **Expansion** — Expands or contracts the outer edge of the mesh in relation to the layer contents.

4  Click to place pins in the mesh at areas you want to transform and at areas you want to remain fixed. To delete a pin, select it and press Delete, or press Alt and click it. To delete all pins, click the Remove all pins button on the options bar.

5  Click to select a pin, and drag it to transform the image.

6  On the options bar, from the Rotate list, select either Fixed or Auto to rotate the mesh based on the selected mode.

7  If desired, rotate the mesh around specific points. To do so, first select the point. Then press Alt and point just outside of the point. When a circle appears, drag to rotate the mesh.

8  When the transformation is finished, press Enter or click the Commit Puppet Warp button.

*Exhibit 5-1: Puppet Warp settings on the options bar*

By using Puppet Warp, you can overlap parts of an image, but you might want part of an image to appear behind, rather than in front of, another part (or vice versa). You can adjust this by selecting a pin and, on the options bar, clicking the Pin Depth buttons.

While the Puppet Warp mesh is visible, you can press Ctrl+Z to undo the last transformation. Because individual transformations don't appear in the History panel, you can't undo more than one transformation. You can, however, undo all transformations by pressing Esc. Once you've committed Puppet Warp transformations, you won't be able to undo them by, for example, moving part of the image that you've overlapped with another part, because these transformations alter the image pixels.

Puppet Warp works best if the image you want to warp is on a separate layer. That way, you can adjust an object without having to pin many other image areas that you want to remain fixed.

**Puppet Warp and portraits**

There are many ways to use Puppet Warp to touch up an image. For example, in a portrait, you could use Puppet Warp to adjust a person's smile or other features. When doing so, you might find it useful to place pins *around* the features you want to adjust, rather than on them. For example, to touch up a person's smile, you might place pins around the mouth, rather than on the mouth, so that when you adjust the pins, you warp the area around the mouth, giving a more natural appearance.

*Do it!*

## A-3:   Using Puppet Warp

The files for this activity are in Student Data folder **Unit 5\Topic A**.

| Here's how | Here's why |
|---|---|
| 1 Open Puppet | |
| Save the image as **My puppet** | In the current topic folder. |
| 2 Select the Manikin layer | If necessary. |
| 3 Choose **Edit, Puppet Warp** | To display a mesh over the layer. |
| On the options bar, from the Density list, select **More Points** | To increase the density of the mesh, allowing for more control over the warp. |
| 4 Observe the mesh | It extends slightly beyond the image |
| On the options bar, edit the Expansion box to read **0** | |
| 5 Observe the pointer | It indicates that clicking will add pins to the image. |
| Click as shown | To add a pin to the manikin's head. When you point to a pin, the pointer changes to indicate that you can drag the pin to warp the mesh. However, you first need to add other pins. |

6 Click to add pins to the indicated areas

7 Click the indicated pin

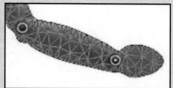

To select it.

From the Rotate list, select **Fixed**

Drag the pin up, as shown

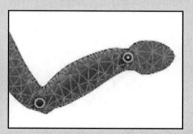

To rotate the manikin's arm at the elbow.

On the options bar, from the Rotate list, select **Auto**

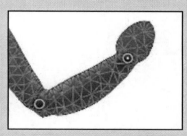

Photoshop automatically adjusts the mesh to compensate for the rotation.

8 Press and hold ⟨ALT⟩ and point just outside of the indicated pin

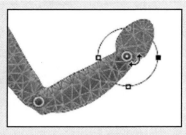

A circle indicates that you can rotate the mesh.

While holding ⟨ALT⟩, drag to rotate the hand, as shown

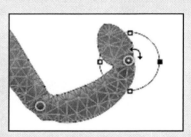

9 Click the manikin's left elbow pin and rotate the arm up toward its head

Press ⟨CTRL⟩ + ⟨Z⟩

As you drag, the elbow moves but the hand stays fixed. You want to rotate the entire arm at the shoulder.

10 Press ⟨ALT⟩ and click the elbow pin

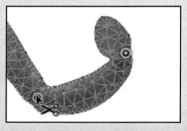

To delete it. The mesh compensates slightly.

11 Click the left hand pin and drag the arm as shown

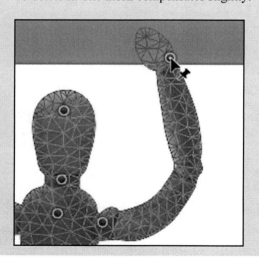

12  Click to add a pin to the elbow
    again

    Drag the hand as shown

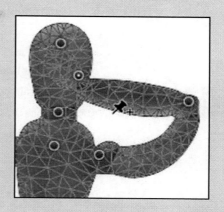

13  Observe the hand    It covers the manikin's head. You want it to
                        appear behind the manikin's head.

    On the options bar, click     (The Pin Depth button.) To move the pin down
                              in the stacking order.

    Observe the hand    It is now behind the manikin's head.

14  On the options bar, from the    To see the effect of this option, which isn't
    Mode list, select **Distort**    appropriate for this image.

    From the Mode list, select **Rigid**    The arm is less distorted than in Normal mode.

15  Press ( ↵ ENTER )    To commit the warp.

16  Update and close the image

# Topic B: Liquify

This topic covers the following ACE exam objectives for Photoshop CS6.

| # | Objective |
|---|---|
| **7.2** | **Working with Liquify** |
| 7.2.1 | Using the Liquify tool for correcting a photographic image or for special effect |
| 7.2.2 | Understanding the Liquify tool with regards to brush size and GPU acceleration |
| 7.2.3 | Understanding Freeze/Thaw |

## The Liquify filter

*Explanation*

By using the Liquify filter, you can transform an image at the pixel level in a number of ways. Although the Puppet Warp tool can be used in much the same way, both tools have individual capabilities that might make one better than the other for a specific task.

To use the Liquify filter, choose Filter, Liquify to open the selected layer or current selection in the Liquify dialog box, shown in Exhibit 5-2. The Liquify filter is useful for touching up photographs a s well as for applying special effects to images. When using it to touch up an image, you'll probably see the best results by using small brush movements, gradually building up the effect of the filter as desired.

The Liquify dialog box contains tools you can use to modify the image in several ways. By default, when you open the Liquify dialog box, only the Forward Warp, Reconstruct, Pucker, Bloat, and Push Left transformation tools are displayed. To see the Twirl Clockwise, Freeze Mask, and Thaw Mask tools, check Advanced Mode.

The following table describes each transformation tool.

| Liquify tool | Description |
|---|---|
| Forward Warp | Stretch and pull pixels in any direction. |
| Reconstruct | Selectively undo and restore distortions. |
| Twirl Clockwise | Twirl pixels in a clockwise direction. (Hold Alt+Shift to twirl counterclockwise.) |
| Pucker | Shrinks and pinches pixels. |
| Bloat | Magnifies and bloats pixels. |
| Push Left | Shifts pixels at a 90° angle to the direction you drag. |
| Freeze Mask | Protects image areas with a mask overlay. |
| Thaw Mask | Erases areas frozen with the Freeze Mask tool. |

The Liquify filter uses OpenGL to enhance performance. If your computer doesn't support OpenGL, you might notice that the filter doesn't perform as well.

*Exhibit 5-2: The Liquify dialog box*

*Do it!*

## B-1: Using the Liquify filter

The files for this activity are in Student Data folder **Unit 5\Topic B**.

| Here's how | Here's why |
|---|---|
| 1 Open Planter 2 | |
| Save the image as **My planter 2** | In the current topic folder. |
| 2 Select the **Background** layer | |
| 3 Choose **Filter, Liquify...** | To open the selected layer in the Liquify dialog box. The Forward Warp tool is selected by default. |
| At the right of the dialog box, check **Advanced Mode** | To make more options available. |
| 4 In the toolbar, click 🖌 | The Freeze Mask tool. |
| Set the Brush Size to **50** | |
| Paint in the image as shown | |
| | To create a freeze mask. |
| 5 Click 🖐 | The Forward Warp tool. |
| Set the Brush Size to **200** | |
| Drag from left ro right across the image | |

6 Click    The Thaw Mask tool.

Set the Brush Size to **100**

Paint in the image as shown

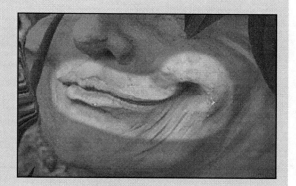

7 Click

Set the Brush Size to **30**

Drag the right corner of the planter's mouth up slightly

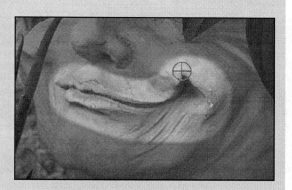

Drag the corner up again toward the mask    The mask prevents the tool from affecting the masked area.

8 Click **OK**    To close the dialog box.

9 Update and close the image

# Topic C: Black and white and duotone images

This topic covers the following ACE exam objectives for Photoshop CS6.

| # | Objective |
|---|-----------|
| **7.8** | **Creating specialty images (black and white and duotone)** |
| 7.8.1 | Best practices for creating black and white and duotone specialty images in Photoshop using Adjustment Layers and the Image > Mode command settings |
| 7.8.2 | Using a Black & White Adjustment layer |
| 7.8.3 | Using the Targeted Adjustment Tool |
| 7.8.4 | Using layer blending |
| 7.8.5 | Using the Channel Mixer |

## The Black & White options

*Explanation*

When you want to display or print a color image in *grayscale*, you can convert it by choosing Image, Mode, Grayscale. However, you can create a grayscale version and have more control over the conversion by using the Black & White options in the Adjustments panel.

When you convert an image to grayscale by choosing Image, Mode, Grayscale, the conversion is based on the image's overall luminosity. However, some channels might contain detail that can provide more contrast in the grayscale version of the image. The Image, Mode, Grayscale command tends to rely more on the Green channel for determining the contrast in the converted image, so if the Red or Blue channels include more detail, then you might get a better grayscale version if you base the conversion more on the Red or Blue channel.

The Black & White commands create a grayscale image based on specific percentages of red, yellow, green, cyan, blue, and magenta. You can choose Image, Adjustments, Black & White to open the Black & White dialog box, but changes made there result in a destructive edit. It's usually better to perform a nondestructive edit instead. To do so, use the Adjustments panel's Black & White options, shown in Exhibit 5-3, to make your changes to an adjustment layer instead of to the original image.

To create a grayscale version of an image by using the Black & White options:

1 In the Channels panel, click each color channel to determine which ones display the best contrast.

2 In the Layers panel, select the layer containing the content you want to display in grayscale.

3 In the Adjustments panel, click the Black & White icon to create an adjustment layer and display the Black & White options.

4 Adjust the color percentages to get the best contrast for the grayscale version. For example, you can use the Targeted Adjustment tool to point to a color and drag to adjust its percentage.

You can achieve different effects by selecting options from the Preset list. You can also apply a tint to an image by checking Tint and specifying Hue and Saturation values.

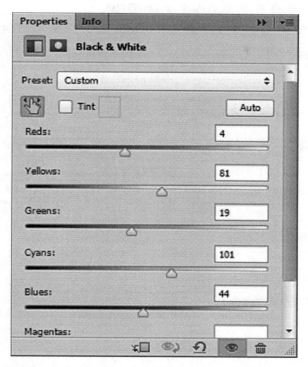

*Exhibit 5-3: The Black & White options in the Properties panel*

The Black & White options don't convert the image to Grayscale mode. Instead, it's displayed as an RGB image with values that generate a grayscale appearance. As you adjust the source color percentages, you must be careful to avoid blowing out the highlights and blocking shadows, both of which would diminish image detail.

**Channel Mixer**

Another method for creating grayscale or tinted images is to use a Channel Mixer adjustment layer. The Channel Mixer adjustment uses the tonal values of color components in an image to modify existing color channels. Rather than adding or subtracting color, the Channel Mixer modifies the grayscale representations of each color channel. To mix color channels:

1   In the Adjustments panel, click the Channel Mixer button.
2   In the Properties panel, from the Output Channel list, select a color channel to modify.
3   Adjust the color sliders as desired.
4   Adjust the Constant slider to modify the grayscale value of the output channel.

You can also use a Channel mixer adjustment layer to create a grayscale image. To do so, add a Channel Mixer adjustment layer and, in the Properties panel, check Monochrome.

*Do it!*

### C-1: Creating a grayscale image

The files for this activity are in Student Data folder **Unit 5\Topic C**.

| Here's how | Here's why |
|---|---|
| 1 Open Eagle 2 | |
| Save the image as **My eagle 2** | (In the current topic folder.) You'll create a duplicate image and convert it to grayscale for comparison with another that you'll convert with a Black & White adjustment layer. |
| 2 Choose **Image, Duplicate...** | To open the Duplicate Image dialog box. |
| Edit the As box to read **My eagle grayscale** | |
| Click **OK** | To open the duplicate image in a new tab. |
| 3 Choose **Image, Mode, Grayscale** | A message box appears, asking whether you want to discard the image's color information. |
| Click **Discard** | To discard the color information. |
| 4 View the My eagle 2 image | You'll specify options for converting the image to black and white. |
| 5 In the Channels panel, view each channel | (Red, green, and blue.) To find the channel with the most contrast in the areas that are important to you. |
| View the RGB channel | |
| 6 In the Adjustments panel, click 🔲 | (The Black & White button.) To create an adjustment layer and to display the Black & White options in the Properties panel. |
| 7 In the Properties panel, click **Auto** | This makes the eagle's beak too dark. |

8  Click ✋                                    The Targeted Adjustment tool.

   Point to the eagle's beak, and
   press and hold the mouse button

The pointer changes to indicate that you can
now drag to adjust the color percentage for the
color you're pointing to.

   Drag to the right                          To increase the Yellow percentage to about 80,
                                              lightening the beak.

9  Using the Targeted Adjustment              To increase the Cyan percentage to about 100.
   tool, point to the left of the eagle's
   beak and drag right

10 Arrange the images so that you             (For example, choose Window, Arrange, 2-up
   can see both of them                       Vertical.) To compare the conversions.

11 Save and close
   My eagle grayscale

   Update My eagle 2

## Grayscale and RGB file size

*Explanation*

After you use a Black & White adjustment layer to display an image as grayscale, the image is still defined as a combination of Red, Green, and Blue channels (RGB Color mode). Because an RGB image uses three channels, and a grayscale image uses only one channel, an RGB image's file size is three times larger than a grayscale version. Therefore, after you use the Black & White command to display an image in grayscale, you should convert the image from RGB to grayscale to reduce the file size. The grayscale version will look identical to the RGB version.

If you applied the Black & White command as an adjustment layer, then when you convert to grayscale, you'll be prompted to either discard the adjustment layer or flatten the image. To maintain its appearance based on the settings you chose for the Black & White adjustment layer, you'll have to flatten the image.

*Do it!*

### C-2: Converting an image from RGB to Grayscale

| Here's how | Here's why |
|---|---|
| 1 From the Document statistics pop-up menu, choose **Document Sizes** | `Doc: 2.39M/3.42M`<br><br>If necessary, click the triangle in the status bar to display the pop-up menu. |
| 2 Choose **Image**, **Mode**, **Grayscale** | An alert dialog box appears. |
| Click **Flatten** | To flatten the image to a single Background layer. |
| In the second alert box, click **Discard** | |
| 3 Observe the image size | `Doc: 817.0K/1.82M`<br><br>The image is significantly smaller. |
| 4 Update the image | |

## Creating duotones

*Explanation*

Although a grayscale image can display 256 levels of gray onscreen, a version printed on a press typically reproduces only about 50 levels of gray. You can add one or more colored inks to generate the image, and this broadens the image's tonal range in the printed version. A grayscale image that is reproduced by using one or more colored inks is called a *duotone*. You can also use a duotone to add visual interest to a grayscale image by tinting it.

Technically, a duotone is a grayscale image that's reproduced by using two inks—often black ink with one colored ink. A grayscale image reproduced with a single color of ink is a monotone. Grayscale images reproduced with three or four inks are tritones or quadtones, respectively. However, all of these variations are often generically referred to as duotones.

To create any of these duotone variations in Photoshop:

1  Open a grayscale image, or convert a color image to grayscale.

2  Choose Image, Mode, Duotone to open the Duotone Options dialog box. You can specify a monotone, duotone, tritone, or quadtone.

3  From the Type list, select the duotone variation you want to use.

4  Next to each ink, click the color swatch to open the Color Libraries dialog box. Specify the color you want to use for the ink, and click OK.

*Do it!*

## C-3: Creating a duotone

| Here's how | Here's why |
|---|---|
| 1 Choose **Image**, **Mode**, **Duotone...** | To open the Duotone Options dialog box. |
| From the Type list, select **Duotone** | |
| 2 Click the color swatch to the right of Ink 2 | To open the Color Picker (Ink 2 Color) dialog box. |
| 3 Click **Color Libraries** | |
| Type **286** | To select PANTONE 286 C. |
| Click **OK** | To return to the Duotone Options dialog box. |
| 4 Click **OK** | Black and Pantone 1665 combine to display the image. |
| 5 Update the image | |

### Duotone curves

*Explanation*

After you convert a grayscale image to a duotone, you can adjust its settings in the Duotone Options dialog box (choose Image, Mode, Duotone). If you want to change how each ink is distributed throughout the image, then in the Duotone Options dialog box, click the curve icon next to an ink color to open the Duotone Curve dialog box. You can adjust each duotone curve by dragging a point on the curve up or down (but not left or right). Click OK to return to the Duotone Options dialog box. You can then adjust another ink's curve, or click OK.

*Do it!*

### C-4:   Adjusting duotone curves

| Here's how | Here's why |
|---|---|
| 1  Choose **Image**, **Mode**, **Duotone...** | To open the Duotone Options dialog box. After looking at the duotone, you decide that the effect is too strong and needs editing. |
| 2  Click the curve icon (the diagonal line) | To open the Duotone Curve dialog box for the Pantone color. |
| 3  Drag the 100% point in the top-right area of the graph down until the 100 box reads **70**, as shown | To lessen the intensity of the ink in the image. |
| 4  Drag the 60% point on the curve down to **35%** | To slightly lessen the intensity in the midtones. |
| Click **OK** | |

5  Edit the Ink 1 curve as shown, with the 80% point dropped down to **75%**

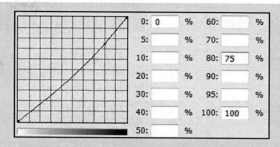

| 0: | 0 | % | 60: | | % |
| 5: | | % | 70: | | % |
| 10: | | % | 80: | 75 | % |
| 20: | | % | 90: | | % |
| 30: | | % | 95: | | % |
| 40: | | % | 100: | 100 | % |
| 50: | | % | | | |

To lighten the dark gray areas, allowing more color to show through and providing more clarity.

Click **OK**    To return to the Duotone Options dialog box.

6  Click **OK**    To return to the image.

7  Update and close the image

# Topic D: Smart Filters

*Explanation*

When you apply a filter to an image, the filter changes the pixel data to which it is applied. However, you can apply a filter nondestructively as a *Smart Filter*. You can then experiment with filter settings without destructively changing the actual image pixel data. Therefore, you can easily modify a filter's effects, or you can remove the filter altogether from the image to return to the original image appearance.

If you want to apply a filter to a layer as a Smart Filter, you must first convert the layer to a Smart Object layer. You can then apply almost any Photoshop filter to the Smart Object layer, and it will be applied as a Smart Filter. You can also apply the Shadow/Highlight and Variations adjustments as Smart Filters. However, you can't apply the following filters as Smart Filters:

- Extract
- Liquify
- Pattern Maker
- Vanishing Point

### Applying a Smart Filter

If the layer to which you want to apply a Smart Filter is not already a Smart Object layer, select it and choose Filter, Convert for Smart Filters. To apply a Smart Filter, select a Smart Object layer, choose a filter, and specify its settings. The Smart Filter then appears in the Layers panel, as shown in Exhibit 5-4.

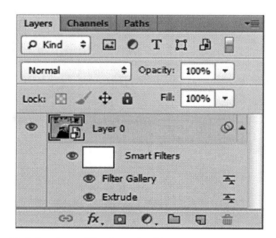

*Exhibit 5-4: The Ripple filter applied as a Smart Filter to a Smart Object layer*

### Editing a Smart Filter

After you apply a Smart Filter, you can edit its effects at any time. Each time you adjust the filter settings, the new settings are applied to the original image data because the Smart Filter is applied nondestructively. To edit a Smart Filter's settings, double-click it in the Layers panel to open the filter's dialog box.

### Removing a Smart Filter

To remove a Smart Filter, drag it to the Delete layer button in the Layers panel. The Smart Filter will be removed and its effects will no longer apply to the image.

*Do it!*

## D-1:   Applying Smart Filters

The files for this activity are in Student Data folder **Unit 5\Topic D**.

| Here's how | Here's why |
|---|---|
| 1  Open Eagle 3 | |
| Save the image as **My eagle 3** | (In the current topic folder.) The image contains a single layer. You'll convert the layer to a Smart Object so you can apply Smart Filters. |
| 2  Choose **Filter**, **Convert for Smart Filters** | A dialog box informs you that the layer will be converted to a Smart Object. |
| Click **OK** | |
| | The layer icon displays a badge to indicate that it's a Smart Object layer. You can now apply filters as Smart Filters. |
| 3  Choose **Filter**, **Filter Gallery...** | |
| Delete any existing filters | (If necessary.) If more than one filter is applied. If one filter remains, you can select another one to replace it. |
| 4  Expand the Artistic category | |
| Select the **Cutout** filter | |
| Click **OK** | |
| | The Smart Filter applies to the entire image. Because you applied this filter as a Smart Filter, you can adjust its settings at any time, and the changes will be based on the original image, rather than on the current filtered version of it. Therefore, you can regain earlier image detail that the filter might have obscured. |
| 5  In the Layers panel, double-click **Filter Gallery** | |
| Set the Edge Simplicity to **0** | |
| Click **OK** | To adjust the Smart Filter. You'll add a second Smart Filter. |

| | |
|---|---|
| 6 Choose **Filter**, **Stylize**, **Extrude...** | To open the Extrude dialog box. |
| Edit the Depth to **15** | |
| Click **OK** | Both Smart Filters are now listed in the Layers panel. |
| 7 Drag the Filter Gallery Smart Filter above the Extrude Smart Filter | 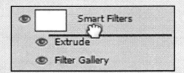 |
| | To change the stacking order. |
| 8 Update the image | |

## Smart Filter masks

*Explanation*

One of the benefits of Smart Filters is that you can easily mask their effects in an image to control which portion of the image displays the filter effect, and you can edit the mask as often as necessary. When you apply a Smart Filter to a Smart Object, a mask thumbnail appears on the Smart Filters line in the Layers panel. By default, the mask thumbnail is white, indicating that the filter's effects apply to the entire layer. You can work with filter masks, using the same techniques you use to work with layer masks. For example, you can paint on a filter mask with black to hide the filter's effects.

Before you apply a Smart Filter, you can select a portion of a Smart Object layer so that when you apply the Smart Filter, it will automatically create a filter mask based on the selection. The filter mask thumbnail displays white to indicate areas where the filter effect will appear, and black to indicate areas where it won't.

*Do it!*

## D-2: Masking Smart Filter effects

| Here's how | Here's why |
|---|---|
| 1 Click the Smart Filters mask thumbnail, as shown | 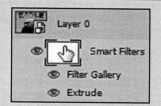 |
| | To select the mask thumbnail so you can edit the mask with painting tools. You'll paint with black to hide parts of the Smart Filter. |
| 2 Select the Brush tool | |
| 3 Press ⓧ | |
| 4 Open the Brush Preset picker<br><br>Select the Soft Round brush | 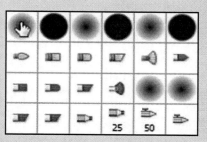 |
| Set the size to approximately **30** | |
| 5 Paint around the eagle | To apply black to the filter mask so that the filter's effect is removed, erasing the horizontal white lines. |
| 6 Observe the filter mask thumbnail |  |
| | The thumbnail is black where you painted around the eagle. The thumbnail is white in the surrounding area, so only that part of the image will display the filter's effects. |
| 7 Hide and show the Smart Filters' effects | Click the eye icon next to Smart Filters in the layers panel. |
| 8 Update and close the image | |

# Unit summary: Creative image effects

*Topic A*  In this topic, you used the Create Warped Text button to **warp** a type layer. You also used the Edit, Transform, Warp command to apply a preset warp and to customize a warp. Then you learned how to use the **Puppet Warp** command.

*Topic B*  In this topic, you learned how to use the **Liquify filter** to modify an image.

*Topic C*  In this topic, you used the Adjustments panel's **Black & White** options to maximize contrast in an image you converted from RGB to grayscale. You also converted a grayscale image to a **duotone**, and you adjusted the curves for individual inks in a duotone image

*Topic D*  In this topic, you converted a layer to a Smart Object, and then you applied a filter as a **Smart Filter**. You also applied a mask to a Smart Filter.

## Review questions

1 True or false? After you apply a warp to type, the text remains editable.

2 Which of the following can you apply to a selection or layer? [Choose all that apply.]

 A A preset warp.

 B A custom warp.

 C A preset warp and a custom warp at the same time.

 D None; you can apply a warp only to an entire layer, not to a selection.

3 While using the Puppet Warp tool, you want to delete a pin. Which of the following are methods you can use to do this? [Choose all that apply.]

 A Select the pin and press Delete.

 B Press Esc.

 C Press Alt and click the pin.

 D Press Ctrl and click the pin.

4 When using the Liquify filter, what tool can you use to protect specific areas of the image?

 A The Freeze Mask tool.

 B The Thaw Mask tool.

 C The Forward Warp tool.

 D The Reconstruct tool.

5 Which command should you choose to have the most control over converting an image from RGB to grayscale?

 A Image, Mode, Grayscale

 B Image, Adjustments, Black & White

 C Image, Mode, Bitmap

 D Image, Adjustments, Desaturate

6 An RGB Color image's file size is _____ the same image converted to Grayscale mode.

  A  Three times larger than

  B  The same as

  C  Six times larger than

  D  One-third the size of

7 Which is not an option for the number of inks you can specify for an image in Duotone mode?

  A  Two

  B  Three

  C  Four

  D  Five

8 For you to create a duotone image, the image must be in _____ mode.

  A  CMYK

  B  RGB

  C  Grayscale

  D  Indexed Color

9 To adjust how each ink in a duotone image is distributed throughout various tonal regions, you should adjust its _____.


10 Which of the following statements are true of Smart Objects? [Choose all that apply.]

  A  A Smart Object can be transformed to a small size and then back to its original size with no loss of quality.

  B  A Smart Object's data cannot be edited after you've converted it from layer data.

  C  Only raster, not vector, data can be stored as a Smart Object.

  D  You can combine multiple layers into one Smart Object.

11 How can you convert several selected layers into a Smart Object?

  A  From the Layers panel menu, choose New Group.

  B  From the Layers panel menu, choose Convert to Smart Object.

  C  From the Layers panel menu, choose New Group from Layers.

  D  From the Layers panel menu, choose Merge Layers.

## Independent practice activity

In this activity, you'll warp text in an image. Then you'll use Puppet Warp and Liquify to modify the image. You'll also convert the image to black and white. Finally, you'll apply a Smart Filter.

The files for this activity are in Student Data folder **Unit 5\Unit summary**.

1 Open Rhino ad 2 and save it as **My rhino ad 2**.

2 Warp the text Pangaea Zoological Park with the **Bulge** style. Modify the warp so that the text doesn't overlap the other type layer.

3 Use Puppet Warp to move the left rhino's ear slightly to the right, affecting as little of the surrounding image as possible. (*Hint*: Adjust the mesh. Also, in addition to placing pins on and around the ear, pin the corners and edges of the image.)

4 Use Liquify to extend the length of the left rhino's horn, without affecting the rest of the image. (*Hint*: Use multiple short strokes.)

5 Apply the Smart Filter of your choice to the Rhinos layer.

6 Convert the image to black and white using the method of your choice.

7 Update and close the image.

# Appendix A

## ACE exam objectives map

This appendix covers these additional topics:

**A** ACE exam objectives for Photoshop CS6, with references to corresponding coverage in ILT Series courseware.

# Topic A: Comprehensive exam objectives

*Explanation*

The following table lists the Adobe Certified Expert (ACE) exam objectives for Photoshop CS6 and indicates where each objective is covered in conceptual explanations, hands-on activities, or both.

## 1.0 Managing assets using Adobe Bridge

| # | Objective | Course level | Conceptual information | Supporting activities |
|---|---|---|---|---|
| **1.1** | **Navigating between Adobe Bridge and your computer** | | | |
| 1.1.1 | Navigating the computer structure using the path bar | Basic | Unit 7, Topic A | A-2 |
| 1.1.2 | Copying and pasting media in Bridge | Basic | Unit 7, Topic A | A-2 |
| 1.1.3 | Browsing subfolder structures | Basic | Unit 7, Topic A | A-2 |
| 1.1.4 | Working with filters | Basic | Unit 7, Topic B | B-2 |
| 1.1.5 | Using Review Mode | Basic | Unit 7, Topic A | A-3 |
| 1.1.6 | Importing images from a camera | Basic | Unit 7, Topic A | A-1 |
| **1.2** | **Working with metadata** | | | |
| 1.2.1 | Viewing, modifying, and replacing metadata in images | Basic | Unit 7, Topic B | B-1 |
| 1.2.2 | Viewing, modifying, and replacing metadata in graphics | Basic | Unit 7, Topic B | B-1 |
| 1.2.3 | Viewing, modifying, and replacing metadata in video | Basic | Unit 7, Topic B | B-1 |
| **1.3** | **Organizing collections** | | | |
| 1.3.1 | Creating collections | Basic | Unit 7, Topic C | C-1 |
| 1.3.2 | Creating Smart collections | Basic | Unit 7, Topic C | C-1 |
| 1.3.3 | Creating Favorites for groups of images and media | Basic | Unit 7, Topic C | |
| **1.4** | **Outputting projects to PDF and for the Web** | | | |
| 1.4.1 | Creating PDF documents and PDF slide shows | Basic | Unit 7, Topic D | D-1 |
| 1.4.2 | Creating HTML and Flash-based Websites | Basic | Unit 7, Topic D | D-2 |
| 1.4.3 | Uploading a Website to a hosting provider by using FTP | Basic | Unit 7, Topic D | D-2 |
| **1.5** | **Automating multiple images in Bridge** | | | |
| 1.5.1 | Using Batch Rename | Production | Unit 1, Topic D | D-6 |
| 1.5.2 | Using the Photoshop Image Processor | Production | Unit 1, Topic D | D-1 |
| 1.5.3 | Calling batch actions from within Photoshop | Production | Unit 1, Topic D | D-5 |
| 1.5.4 | Using Merge to HDR Pro | Production | Unit 2, Topic B | |
| 1.5.5 | Differentiating between using Camera Raw in Bridge versus using Camera Raw and Photoshop | Production | Unit 1, Topic C | |

## 2.0 Using Camera Raw

| # | Objective | Course level | Conceptual information | Supporting activities |
|---|-----------|--------------|------------------------|-----------------------|
| **2.1** | **Basic single image adjustment** | | | |
| 2.1.1 | Determining the correct white balance for an image | Production | Unit 1, Topic A | A-1 |
| 2.1.2 | Adjusting exposure and contrast | Production | Unit 1, Topic A | A-2 |
| 2.1.3 | Understanding the differences between clarity, vibrance, and saturation | Production | Unit 1, Topic A | A-3 |
| 2.1.4 | Determining the benefits of Raw format and limitations of saving images as JPG | Production | Unit 1, Topic A | |
| **2.2** | **Selective image corrections** | | | |
| 2.2.1 | Successfully applying a local correction to an image and modifying the selection using Camera Raw tools | Production | Unit 1, Topic B | B-1 |
| 2.2.2 | Using Targeted Adjustment tools | Production | Unit 1, Topic B | B-2 |
| 2.2.3 | Using the Graduated Filter tool | Production | Unit 1, Topic B | B-3 |
| **2.3** | **Batch processing and editing** | | | |
| 2.3.1 | Syncing develop settings in Camera Raw | Production | Unit 1, Topic C | C-3 |
| 2.3.2 | Processing JPG images in Camera Raw and Photoshop | Production | Unit 1, Topic B | B-1 |
| 2.3.3 | Defining edit presets | Production | Unit 1, Topic C | C-1 |
| **2.4** | **Understanding Process Version and workflow options** | | | |
| 2.4.1 | Understanding the differences between Process Version 2010 and 2012 | Production | Unit 1, Topic A | |
| 2.4.2 | Explaining the purpose of Process Version and how it applies to the development of images in Camera Raw | Production | Unit 1, Topic A | |
| **2.5** | **Automating multiple images** | | | |
| 2.5.1 | Development of presets and snapshots | Production | Unit 1, Topic C | C-1 |
| 2.5.2 | Applying presets to single and multiple images | Production | Unit 1, Topic C | C-1 |
| 2.5.3 | Exporting image settings to use in another computer | Production | Unit 1, Topic C | |

## 3.0 Understanding Photoshop fundamentals

| # | Objective | Course level | Conceptual information | Supporting activities |
|---|---|---|---|---|
| **3.1** | **Navigating the Photoshop workspace** | | | |
| 3.1.1 | Zooming and moving around an image in Photoshop | Basic | Unit 1, Topic B | B-3 |
| 3.1.2 | Setting up guides, rulers, and grid units | Basic | Unit 1, Topic B | B-4 |
| 3.1.3 | Using keyboard shortcuts to temporarily select tools | Basic | Unit 1, Topic B | B-3 |
| 3.1.4 | Selecting, modifying, and replacing Photoshop workspace and keyboard shortcuts | Basic | Unit 1, Topic B | B-2 |
| 3.1.5 | Understanding the Application frame | Basic | Unit 1, Topic B | B-1 |
| **3.2** | **Importing and exporting presets** | | | |
| 3.2.1 | Knowing the location of preset files on both a PC and Mac platform | Basic | Unit 1, Topic C | |
| 3.2.2 | Understanding the process of exporting and importing presets | Basic | Unit 1, Topic C | C-2 |
| **3.3** | **Resetting sliders and options** | | | |
| 3.3.1 | Working with sliders and buttons | Basic | Unit 1, Topic C | C-1 |
| 3.3.2 | Using Alt key combinations | Basic | Unit 1, Topic C | |
| 3.3.3 | Resetting parameters | Basic | Unit 1, Topic C | C-2 |
| 3.3.4 | Using Shift modifiers | Basic | Unit 1, Topic C | C-1 |
| **3.4** | **Using tool groups and options** | | | |
| 3.4.1 | Selecting tools from a tool group | Basic | Unit 2, Topic A | A-1 |
| 3.4.2 | Modifying individual tool options | Basic | Unit 1, Topic C | C-1 |
| 3.4.3 | Creating tool presets | Basic | Unit 1, Topic C | C-1 |

## 4.0  Understanding selections

| # | Objective | Course level | Conceptual information | Supporting activities |
|---|-----------|--------------|------------------------|-----------------------|
| **4.1** | **Creating selections using appropriate tools** | | | |
| 4.1.1 | Creating selections with various tools and determining which selection tools work best for a given situation | Basic | Unit 2, Topic A | A-1, A-2 |
| 4.1.2 | Working with the Quick Selection tool and options | Basic | Unit 2, Topic A | A-3 |
| **4.2** | **Adding and subtracting from selections** | | | |
| 4.2.1 | Adding and subtracting selections | Basic | Unit 2, Topic B | B-1 |
| 4.2.2 | Adding and subtracting of selections using different selection tools | Basic | Unit 2, Topic B | B-1 |
| 4.2.3 | Modifying selections | Basic | Unit 2, Topic B | B-2 |
| **4.3** | **Quick Mask usage** | | | |
| 4.3.1 | Creating a Quick Mask from a selection | Advanced | Unit 3, Topic A | A-1 |
| 4.3.2 | Creating a blank Quick Mask | Advanced | Unit 3, Topic A | |
| 4.3.3 | Changing overlay | Advanced | Unit 3, Topic A | |
| 4.3.4 | Using brushes for addition to Quick Mask | Advanced | Unit 3, Topic A | A-1 |
| 4.3.5 | Saving selections | Advanced | Unit 3, Topic A | A-2 |
| **4.4** | **Using Refine Edge** | | | |
| 4.4.1 | Adjusting feather and smart radius | Advanced | Unit 3, Topic C | C-1 |
| 4.4.2 | Masking to new layers or new channels | Advanced | Unit 3, Topic C | C-1 |
| 4.4.3 | Determining which images will best be served by Refine Edge | Advanced | Unit 3, Topic C | C-1 |
| 4.4.4 | Creating selections that will best benefit from Refine Edge | Advanced | Unit 3, Topic C | C-1 |

# 5.0 Understanding layers

| # | Objective | Course level | Conceptual information | Supporting activities |
|---|---|---|---|---|
| **5.1** | **Creating and organizing layers** | | | |
| 5.1.1 | Creating different types of layers and dragging under/over for visibility | Basic | Unit 3, Topic A | A-1, A-2, A-3 |
| 5.1.2 | Hiding and showing layers | Basic | Unit 3, Topic A | A-1 |
| 5.1.3 | Using keyboard shortcuts for moving and creating layers | Basic | Unit 3, Topic A | A-1, A-3 |
| 5.1.4 | Dragging and dropping images between documents | Basic | Unit 3, Topic A | A-2 |
| **5.2** | **Understanding the differences between raster and shape layers** | | | |
| 5.2.1 | Understanding vector layers in Photoshop | Advanced | Unit 4, Topic A | A-2 |
| 5.2.2 | Understanding the benefits of vector layers | Advanced | Unit 4, Topic A | A-1, A-2 |
| 5.2.3 | Comparing and contrasting raster vs. vector | Advanced | Unit 4, Topic A | A-1 |
| **5.3** | **Understanding layer masks** | | | |
| 5.3.1 | Creating layer masks using Panels and shortcuts | Advanced | Unit 3, Topic B | B-1 |
| 5.3.2 | Modifying layer masks using brush-based tools | Advanced | Unit 3, Topic B | B-2, B-4 |
| 5.3.3 | Copying and moving layer masks | Advanced | Unit 3, Topic B | B-2 |
| 5.3.4 | Understanding the relationship between layer masks and Quick Mask | Advanced | Unit 3, Topic B | |
| 5.3.5 | Using layer masks with vector images and type | Advanced | Unit 3, Topic B | B-3 |
| **5.4** | **Searching for layers** | | | |
| 5.4.1 | Organizing documents that have many layers | Advanced | Unit 1, Topic A | |
| 5.4.2 | Using the layer search feature | Advanced | Unit 1, Topic A | A-3 |
| **5.5** | **Understanding layer groups** | | | |
| 5.5.1 | Grouping Layers | Advanced | Unit 1, Topic A | A-1 |
| 5.5.2 | Clipping Layers | Advanced | Unit 1, Topic A | A-2 |
| 5.5.3 | Blend mode and masks using layer groups | Advanced | Unit 1, Topic A | |
| 5.5.4 | Considerations for designs when using layer groups | Advanced | Unit 1, Topic A | |
| 5.5.5 | Keyboard shortcuts for grouping layers | Advanced | Unit 1, Topic A | A-1 |
| **5.6** | **Understanding layer blend modes** | | | |
| 5.6.1 | Toggling blend modes using keyboard shortcuts | Advanced | Unit 1, Topic B | B-1 |
| 5.6.2 | Explanation of blend mode functions and usage | Advanced | Unit 1, Topic B | B-1 |
| 5.6.3 | Blend modes as they apply to video and design | Production | Unit 6, Topic A | |

# 6.0  Understanding adjustments

| # | Objective | Course level | Conceptual information | Supporting activities |
|---|---|---|---|---|
| **6.1** | **Differentiating between adjustment types** | | | |
| 6.1.1 | Identifying the strengths and weaknesses of specific adjustments | Basic | Unit 4, Topic A | A-1, A-2, A-3 |
| | | Advanced | Unit 2, Topic C | C-3, C-4 |
| 6.1.2 | Applying adjustment layers for dramatic effect or color correction | Basic | Unit 4, Topic A<br>Unit 4, Topic B | A-1<br>B-1 |
| | | Advanced | Unit 2, Topic C | C-3, C-4 |
| 6.1.3 | Blending adjustment types | Advanced | Unit 2, Topic C | C-3 |
| **6.2** | **Using TAT, clipping, and visibility** | | | |
| 6.2.1 | Working with the TAT | Basic | Unit 4, Topic B | B-2 |
| **6.3** | **Refining masks on adjustments** | | | |
| 6.3.1 | Refining masks using the Density, Mask Edge, and Refine Mask options found in the Mask Properties panel | Advanced | Unit 3, Topic B | B-2 |

# 7.0  Editing images

| # | Objective | Course level | Conceptual information | Supporting activities |
|---|---|---|---|---|
| **7.1** | **Working with the retouching tools** | | | |
| 7.1.1 | Using Dodge, Burn, Smudge, Blur | Basic | Unit 5, Topic B | B-1, B-2 |
| 7.1.2 | Edge smoothing techniques | Basic | Unit 5, Topic B | B-2 |
| 7.1.3 | Using the Clone Stamp, History Brush, and Sponge | Basic | Unit 5, Topic B | B-4, B-5 |
| **7.2** | **Working with Liquify** | | | |
| 7.2.1 | Using the Liquify tool for correcting a photographic image or for special effect | Advanced | Unit 5, Topic B | B-1 |
| 7.2.2 | Understanding the Liquify tool with regards to brush size and GPU acceleration | Advanced | Unit 5, Topic B | |
| 7.2.3 | Understanding Freeze/Thaw | Advanced | Unit 5, Topic B | B-1 |
| **7.3** | **Using the transform controls** | | | |
| 7.3.1 | Using the transform controls to scale, rotate, and copy images | Basic | Unit 3, Topic B | B-1, B-2 |
| 7.3.2 | Using keyboard modifier combinations for effective usage | Basic | Unit 3, Topic B | B-1 |
| **7.4** | **Using Puppet Warp** | | | |
| 7.4.1 | Using the Puppet Warp tool to correct image problems in people and landscape-based images | Advanced | Unit 5, Topic A | A-3 |
| 7.4.2 | Understanding how to add/removal points | Advanced | Unit 5, Topic A | A-3 |
| 7.4.3 | Understanding the increase/decrease of mesh for maximum effective use | Advanced | Unit 5, Topic A | A-3 |

| # | Objective | Course level | Conceptual information | Supporting activities |
|---|-----------|--------------|------------------------|----------------------|
| **7.5** | **Using the Clone Source panel** | | | |
| 7.5.1 | Understanding how to the use the clone source tool | Basic | Unit 5, Topic B | B-4 |
| 7.5.2 | Understanding horizontal vertical offsets | Basic | Unit 5, Topic B | |
| 7.5.3 | Understanding rotation | Basic | Unit 5, Topic B | |
| 7.5.4 | Cloning images from separate documents | Basic | Unit 5, Topic B | |
| **7.6** | **Creating panoramas** | | | |
| 7.6.1 | Creating panoramas effectively by understanding Perspective, Cylindrical, Reposition, and other layers | Production | Unit 2, Topic A | A-1 |
| 7.6.2 | Understanding geometric distortion correction and layer blending | Production | Unit 2, Topic A | A-1 |
| 7.6.3 | Understanding the Adaptive Wide angle tool and its use in extreme panoramic and wide angle lens scenarios | Production | Unit 2, Topic A | A-2 |
| **7.7** | **Using HDR Pro** | | | |
| 7.7.1 | Best practices for HDR generation | Production | Unit 2, Topic B | B-1 |
| 7.7.2 | 32-bit HDR creation | Production | Unit 2, Topic B | B-1 |
| 7.7.3 | Tone control usage | Production | Unit 2, Topic B | B-1, B-2 |
| 7.7.4 | Developing presets | Production | Unit 2, Topic B | B-2 |
| 7.7.5 | Using ghosting source image alignment and post processing of the image | Production | Unit 2, Topic B | B-1, B-2 |
| **7.8** | **Creating specialty images (black and white and duotone)** | | | |
| 7.8.1 | Best practices for creating black and white and duotone specialty images in Photoshop using Adjustment Layers and the Image > Mode command settings | Advanced | Unit 5, Topic C | C-1, C-3, C-4 |
| 7.8.2 | Using a Black & White Adjustment layer | Advanced | Unit 5, Topic C | C-1 |
| 7.8.3 | Using the Targeted Adjustment Tool | Advanced | Unit 5, Topic C | C-1 |
| 7.8.4 | Using layer blending | Advanced | Unit 5, Topic C | |
| 7.8.5 | Using the Channel Mixer | Advanced | Unit 5, Topic C | |
| **7.9** | **Selecting color** | | | |
| 7.9.1 | Best practices for selecting color in an image and working with the appropriate color adjustment tools to isolate color casts for removal | Advanced | Unit 2, Topic C | C-1, C-2, C-3 |
| 7.9.2 | Creating single color images and spot color designs | Advanced | Unit 2, Topic C | C-4, C-5 |
| 7.9.3 | Adjusting colors that are out of gamut | Basic | Unit 5, Topic D | D-1 |

# 8.0 Working with design and print production

| # | Objective | Course level | Conceptual information | Supporting activities |
|---|-----------|--------------|------------------------|----------------------|
| **8.1** | **Using character and paragraph styles** | | | |
| 8.1.1 | Creating and modifying character and paragraph styles | Basic | Unit 3, Topic C | C-3 |
| 8.1.2 | Best practices for creating reusable styles | Basic | Unit 3, Topic C | |
| 8.1.3 | Clearing style formats from a documents | Basic | Unit 3, Topic C | |
| 8.1.4 | Font usage considerations | Basic | Unit 3, Topic C | |
| 8.1.5 | OpenType considerations | Basic | Unit 3, Topic C | |
| **8.2** | **Using vector shapes** | | | |
| 8.2.1 | Creating and modifying vector shapes | Advanced | Unit 4, Topic B | B-4 |
| 8.2.2 | Modifying stroke and fill | Advanced | Unit 4, Topic B | B-5 |
| 8.2.3 | Creating pen-based shapes | Advanced | Unit 4, Topic B | B-1, B-3 |
| 8.2.4 | Stroking a path | Advanced | Unit 4, Topic B | B-5 |
| 8.2.5 | Appending and inserting custom shapes | Advanced | Unit 4, Topic B | B-4 |
| **8.3** | **Working with layer comps** | | | |
| 8.3.1 | Creating layer comps | Advanced | Unit 1, Topic D | D-1 |
| 8.3.2 | Specifying what changes in a layer comp | Advanced | Unit 1, Topic D | D-1 |
| 8.3.3 | Updating changes in layer comps | Advanced | Unit 1, Topic D | D-1 |
| **8.4** | **Creating frame based animations** | | | |
| 8.4.1 | Specifying looping | Production | Unit 5, Topic C | C-1, C-4 |
| 8.4.2 | Exporting frame based animations | Production | Unit 5, Topic C | C-4 |
| **8.5** | **Working with layer styles** | | | |
| 8.5.1 | Accessing layer styles from multiple areas in Photoshop | Basic | Unit 3, Topic D | D-2 |
| 8.5.2 | Adding several styles threaded together to create a specific style | Basic | Unit 3, Topic D | D-2 |

## 9.0 Working with video

| # | Objective | Course level | Conceptual information | Supporting activities |
|---|---|---|---|---|
| **9.1** | **Ingesting video into Photoshop** | | | |
| 9.1.1 | Specifying supported video types | Production | Unit 6, Topic A | A-1 |
| 9.1.2 | Tagging and metadata inspection of media images | Production | Unit 6, Topic A | |
| 9.1.3 | Creating video layers | Production | Unit 6, Topic A | A-2 |
| **9.2** | **Cutting and trimming video** | | | |
| 9.2.1 | Using the Trim and Scrub feature | Production | Unit 6, Topic B | B-1, B-2 |
| 9.2.2 | Specifying optimal sizes for playback, audio usage and fade/mute of audio | Production | Unit 6, Topic B | B-4 |
| **9.3** | **Creating transitions within clips** | | | |
| 9.3.1 | Creating transitions between movie clips and other assets in a Photoshop video file | Production | Unit 6, Topic C | C-1 |
| 9.3.2 | Explain cross transition to design elements, blending, layer stack usage, trimming, and effect transitions | Production | Unit 6, Topic C | C-1 |
| **9.4** | **Adding design elements into video** | | | |
| 9.4.1 | Adding graphics | Production | Unit 6, Topic D | D-1 |
| 9.4.2 | Adding text layers for titling | Production | Unit 6, Topic D | D-2 |
| 9.4.3 | Working with 3D elements and textures for use in video | Production | Unit 6, Topic D | |
| 9.4.4 | Understanding the differences between video timelines and regular layers | Production | Unit 6, Topic D | |
| 9.4.5 | Considerations when using ripple delete | Production | Unit 6, Topic D | |
| 9.4.6 | Keyframing events | Production | Unit 6, Topic D | D-4 |
| **9.5** | **Exporting and publishing video** | | | |
| 9.5.1 | Using Adobe Media Encoder | Production | Unit 6, Topic D | E-2 |
| 9.5.2 | Specifying a preset | Production | Unit 6, Topic D | E-2 |
| 9.5.3 | Using a built in preset for upload to commercial site | Production | Unit 6, Topic D | E-2 |
| 9.5.4 | Using Photoshop Image Sequence | Production | Unit 6, Topic D | |
| 9.5.5 | Using the DPX Format | Production | Unit 6, Topic D | |
| **9.6** | **Using LUT adjustments for style** | | | |
| 9.6.1 | Defining Color Look Up Tables (LUT) | Production | Unit 6, Topic E | E-1 |
| 9.6.2 | Explain how the LUT applies to images and video in Photoshop | Production | Unit 6, Topic E | |
| 9.6.3 | Explain how to import LUT files for use in Photoshop | Production | Unit 6, Topic E | |

# 10.0 Outputting for Web, print, and mobile

| # | Objective | Course level | Conceptual information | Supporting activities |
|---|-----------|--------------|------------------------|----------------------|
| **10.1** | **Differentiating between file types** | | | |
| 10.1.1 | Understanding the differences between TIF, JPG, PNG, GIF, PSD, PSB, and other file types | Basic | Unit 1, Topic A | A-1. A-2 |
| 10.1.2 | Understanding which file type to choose for a given scenario | Basic | Unit 1, Topic A | A-1, A-2 |
| **10.2** | **Using Save For Web** | | | |
| 10.2.1 | Using Save For Web for clearing metadata | Production | Unit 5, Topic A | A-1, A-4 |
| 10.2.2 | .Applying color profiles | Production | Unit 5, Topic A | A-4 |
| 10.2.3 | Specifying file sizes | Production | Unit 5, Topic A | A-2, A-6 |
| 10.2.4 | 2 up 4 up comparisons | Production | Unit 5, Topic A | A-4 |
| 10.2.5 | Considerations regarding speed and download for images on the Web | Production | Unit 5, Topic A | A-1, A-3 |
| **10.3** | **Using the Print dialog** | | | |
| 10.3.1 | Setting up appropriate color spaces for proofing | Production | Unit 3, Topic C | C-2 |
| 10.3.2 | Using ICC profiles | Production | Unit 3, Topic C | C-1, C-2, C-3 |
| 10.3.3 | Creating custom paper types | Production | Unit 3, Topic C | C-1, C-2 |
| 10.3.4 | Selecting the appropriate rendering intent | Production | Unit 3, Topic C | C-2 |
| 10.3.5 | Checking for out of gamut colors | Production | Unit 3, Topic C | C-2 |
| 10.3.6 | Simulating black ink | Production | Unit 3, Topic C | C-1 |

# Course summary

This summary contains information to help you bring the course to a successful conclusion. Using this information, you will be able to:

**A** Use the summary text to reinforce what you've learned in class.

**B** Determine the next courses in this series (if any), as well as any other resources that might help you continue to learn about Adobe Photoshop CS6.

# Topic A:  Course summary

Use the following summary text to reinforce what you've learned in class.

## Unit summaries

### Unit 1

In this unit, you learned how to create **layer groups** and how to apply a **clipping mask** to a layer to control visibility. You also learned how to **filter** layers. Next, you applied **blending modes** to layers. You also converted layers to **Smart Objects** and transformed them. Finally, you created and exported **layer comps**.

### Unit 2

In this unit, you added colors to the **Swatches panel** and used fill shortcuts to fill selections and layers with color. In addition, you created **fill layers**. Next, you learned how to use the Gradient tool to add a **gradient** to a layer or selection and how to create a **gradient fill layer**. You also learned how to use **overlay layer styles**. You selected color by using the **Magic Wand** tool and the **Color Range** command, used the Adjustments panel to change an image's **hue** and **saturation** and adjust **vibrance**, used the Hue/Saturation dialog box to **colorize** an image, and created a **spot-color channel**. Finally, you **replaced colors** throughout an image by using the Color Replacement tool.

### Unit 3

In this unit, you painted in **Quick Mask mode** to add to and subtract from a selection and learned how to **save and load** selections. You also created a **layer mask** to hide part of a layer. Then you used the **Horizontal Type Mask** tool to create a mask from text and created a **grayscale mask** to partially mask a portion of an image. Finally, you used the **Refine Edge** dialog box to modify a selection.

### Unit 4

In this unit, you learned about the benefits of using **vector layers** and how vector layers differ from raster layers. You also learned about the uses of **vector paths** in Photoshop. Next, you learned how to use the **Pen tools** to draw paths, and you **converted selections to paths**. You also **saved paths** by using the Paths panel. In addition, you added **vector shapes** to an image and created **brush strokes** that flowed along the shape of a path. Then you used the Direct Selection tool to **edit paths**, you added and removed anchor points, and you created **subpaths**. Finally, you **converted type to paths** and wrapped type along a path.

### Unit 5

In this unit, you used the Create Warped Text button to **warp** a type layer, and you used the Edit, Transform, Warp command to apply a preset warp and to customize a warp. Then you learned how to use the **Puppet Warp** command. Next, you learned how to use the **Liquify filter** to modify an image. You also used the Adjustments panel's **Black & White** options to maximize contrast in an image converted from RGB to grayscale, converted a grayscale image to a **duotone**, and adjusted the curves for individual inks in a duotone image. Finally, you converted a layer to a Smart Object and applied a filter as a **Smart Filter**.

# Topic B: Continued learning after class

It is impossible to learn how to use any software effectively in a single day. To get the most out of this class, students should begin working with Photoshop CS6 to perform real tasks as soon as possible. We also offer resources for continued learning.

## Next courses in this series

This is the second course in this series. The next course in this series is:

- *Photoshop CS6: Production, ACE Edition*

## Other resources

For more information on this and other topics, go to **www.Crisp360.com**.

Crisp360 is an online community where you can expand your knowledge base, connect with other professionals, and purchase individual training solutions.

# Glossary

**Alpha channel**

An additional channel that does not contribute to the image itself, as do color channels.

**Anchor points**

Points that a vector path flows through, much like the dots in a connect-the-dots drawing.

**Clipping mask**

A mask that uses the content of one layer to hide part of the content in another layer. The transparent space in the layer below specifies the areas that are masked in the layer above.

**Clipping path**

A vector path that determines which parts of an image should be transparent when the image is placed in a document in another application.

**Compositing**

Combining multiple images, often for the purpose of creating a new, realistic-looking image.

**Corner point**

An anchor point on a vector path in which two segments flow in different directions. The direction points for a corner point don't have to face exactly opposite one another.

**Direction point**

A point that extends from an anchor point on a vector path and determines the curvature of the adjoining segment.

**Fill layer**

A special type of layer that can contain a solid color, a gradient, or a pattern, and that automatically expands to fill the image if you change its canvas size.

**Flatness value**

A value that designates how many small straight segments a PostScript printer should use in simulating a smooth curve. The higher the value, the fewer the segments.

**Gradient**

A blend of two or more colors in which the colors fade gradually from one to another.

**Group**

A container in the Layers panel that can store multiple layers so you can manipulate them together and collapse them to one item in the panel.

**HSB color model**

A three-channel color model that defines colors based on their hue, saturation, and brightness.

**Layer mask**

A grayscale component that's added to a layer to designate each pixel's visibility. A black pixel in a layer mask makes the corresponding image pixel invisible; a white layer-mask pixel makes the image pixel fully visible.

**Masking**

Selecting pixels for the purpose of partially or fully obscuring them from view.

**Overlay**

A fill, gradient, or pattern applied to a layer through a layer style.

**Quick Mask mode**

A mode that displays a selection as a semi-transparent overlay to help you differentiate between selected and non-selected image areas.

**Segment**

The part of a vector path between two anchor points.

**Shape layer**

A layer consisting of a fill and a vector mask, which creates the appearance of a filled shape within the mask's edges.

**Smart Filter**

A filter applied to a Smart Object layer so that the filter is applied nondestructively.

**Smart Object**

An object that acts as a layer but stores the original image data of one or more layers. Smart Objects allow you to transform an image to smaller sizes and then back to the original size with no loss in quality.

**Smooth point**

An anchor point on a vector path in which the segments on either side curve in the same direction. Smooth points have direction points that face exactly opposite one another.

**Subpath**

A secondary path created along with another path in the Paths panel. Subpaths can add to, subtract from, intersect with, or exclude original path areas, depending on the option selected.

**Swatch**

A color saved in the Swatches panel.

**Vector mask**

A vector path component added to a layer to designate each pixel's visibility, much like a layer mask does.

**Vector path**

A geometric shape, such as a smoothly flowing curve, defined by a series of points with segments between them.

**Warp**

A transformation you can apply to text or image layers that reshapes the content. You can create warps based on preset shapes or by dragging handles.

**Work paths**

Paths that make no visible change in the image but can be used to create vector paths, selections, or clipping paths

# Index